MY UNFURLING

MY UNFURLING

Emerging from the Grip of Anxiety,
Self-Doubt, and Drinking

LISA MAY BENNETT

To request permissions, contact the publisher at lisa@lisamaybennett.com

Paperback ISBN: 979-8-9858750-0-3

Ebook ISBN: 979-8-9858750-1-0

First edition, March 2022

Cover design by Mary Ann Smith

Layout by R.W. Harrison

www.lisamaybennett.com

This book is dedicated to all the late bloomers

Contents

Four
Dormancy

Five
Second Bloom

Six
Tending My Garden

Do not stop thinking of life as an adventure. You have no security unless you can live bravely, excitingly, imaginatively; unless you can choose a challenge instead of competence.
— Eleanor Roosevelt,
The Autobiography of Eleanor Roosevelt

∞

Write the tale that scares you, that makes you feel uncertain, that isn't comfortable. I dare you.
— Michaela Coel,
from her 2021 Emmy Awards acceptance speech

Introduction

I am curled up in the back seat of my car. Beads of sweat cover my face, and I'm trembling. A stabbing pain slices through my gut. The car door by my head is slightly ajar because I might need to lean out and hurl at any second. How much time has gone by since I darted out of the office? Have my coworkers noticed that I'm missing? I am ashamed and furious with myself. Here I am in my late forties, and I still drink enough—on a work night no less—to cause debilitating hangovers. At *any* age, this predicament would be embarrassing. At middle age, it's a big neon sign screaming, "Something's got to change!"

How did I get here? I used to pose that question whenever I disappointed myself. Hangovers were not the only occasion for such self-flagellation. Lying around all weekend watching TV and scrolling on my phone or letting another gym membership lapse made me wonder why I was so weak-willed. Reading a book by a gifted author reminded me that I was falling short of my potential—or, even worse, that I had over-estimated my potential in the first place.

The question of how I got there was rhetorical. I wanted to

wallow in self-loathing and pity; the trickier task of real intro-spection was not so enticing.

A couple of years after that hellacious hangover (and other subsequent benders), I decided to make some changes. I launched a blog. Started moving my body more. Stopped drinking. Looked around for adventure. Signed up for a pricey six-month class to push myself to write.

After decades of being tightly wound, I was going through an unfurling, and it was exhilarating. I danced in the kitchen. Woke up at five o'clock in the morning to write. Tried aerial yoga, zip-lining, Pilates, and flotation therapy. I was alive and hungry and happy.

In that writing class, I created a book proposal in which I argued that feminist leaders and organizations should take up the issue of women and alcohol. I believed then (and still do) that drinking hampers women's potential in a society where we are already at a disadvantage.

However, anointing myself as an expert on the topic didn't feel quite right. I hadn't made the effort to figure out what had happened to me—thus, I didn't possess the assuredness to stand behind what I was writing. I put that proposal away and carried on with my unfurling.

Eventually the questions returned: Why had I been stuck for so long? What was behind my drinking, my penchant for procrastination, and my attachment to distraction? My self-doubt was clearly at the root of many of my issues. How had it become so domineering?

Maybe it's time to revive my book, I mused, but this time I'll use the writing process to *form* a theory rather than starting out with one. My energy, curiosity, and promise as a writer had been stymied, and I was going to explore how this obstruction had happened on my watch.

Early on, I realized there was another query: Who the heck am I, anyway? Writing this memoir became a parallel search for my authentic self.

As I pieced together my story, I hoped that one day it would mark the way for someone else, or at least let others know that they're not alone. But first I had to write with the knowledge that this book might never leave my laptop. I had to be okay with the possibility that these words were just for me.

For months, I wrote whatever came to mind when I sat down at my desk. I didn't follow an outline; I let it flow. When I was done with a topic—such as shoplifting or body image—I wrote the subject on a Post-it Note and placed it on a large whiteboard.

The notes multiplied, arranging themselves into a series of colorful pathways that spiraled outward, representing a life that widened, turned in on itself, and then unfolded again.

The entry point was my mother. I could not even begin to understand myself without examining the sensitive and erratic woman who had raised me.

Over the course of a year, my mom and I recorded a series of conversations about her childhood and what it was like to become a single mom in 1965. I learned more about my grandparents and uncles, glimpsing how the family dynamic that my mom experienced as a girl and young woman had trickled down to me.

The first section of *My Unfurling* looks at those early years inside our loving and religious home, where the seeds of my self-judgment and doubt were first planted.

As my world expanded beyond our four walls, my inner critic sprouted. The second section tells the story of my challenges in school as a late bloomer and my close friendships, which both wounded and saved me.

By early adulthood, my insecurity was well entrenched. In the third section, I reflect on my burgeoning need for love and validation and how I sought this affirmation through romance, sex, and work.

The worst of my tendencies and near-addictions grew like vines, winding themselves around virtually every aspect of my life. The fourth section addresses how I became absorbed in drinking, obsessive-compulsive thoughts and behaviors, and other self-destructive inclinations.

Section five traces my gradual journey out of this tangle. (Spoiler alert: This process will never be fully complete—it is a lifelong practice!)

Finally, section six reviews the values that serve as my new foundation, the practices that have been working, and the self that I uncovered and came to love during this process.

Writing this book included digging through file cabinets, boxes, and bookshelves. I unearthed countless photos, scrapbooks, half-filled journals, assignments from my years as a college writing major, a workbook I kept for a course called Writing as a Means of Self-Discovery, a handful of short stories I drafted in my twenties and thirties, and loose pages with scribbled reflections and tipsy epiphanies.

As you read My Unfurling, you will likely notice my affection for television, movies, music, magazines, and popular culture in general. My love of actors, rock icons, fictional heroes, and juicy plots often led me to dream of being a larger-than-life character myself. I had fun shaping these yearnings into "personas" and sprinkling them throughout the book.

Part of me was nervous that people would think my memoir is one long whine of a privileged white woman with no serious problems. What if I hadn't suffered enough? What if my troubles were boring? I had worked on social justice issues for a nonprofit organization for eighteen years, and now my writing felt trivial and insular by comparison.

I had to reject those thoughts, because deep inside I knew that my evolution mattered, and not only to me. We should consider it a human right to expose the pain and fear beneath our coping mechanisms, to learn from our past, and to compassionately interrogate the thoughts and actions that hold us in place.

Emotional growth spurts make us kinder and more effective advocates for ourselves and others. I contend that the world will be a better place once we all accept that self-exploration does not mark us as soft or egotistical. Perhaps my writing can play a small part in this shift.

On the chalkboard at one of my former gyms, a trainer wrote "Your comfort zone" and drew a circle around it. Far outside the circle they wrote, "Where the magic happens."

Avoiding risk and uncertainty is part of human nature. Not taking a chance often feels like a wise decision. Staying inside one's comfort zone is easy but unfulfilling, safe but stagnant.

So much magic was buried inside me, and by quitting drinking, writing *My Unfurling*, and taking so many other, smaller steps, I finally found a way to bring that magic into the light.

A quick note about alcohol use and recovery:

Central to my story is the decision to remove alcohol from my life. I did not attend Alcoholics Anonymous (AA) meetings or work the Twelve Steps, and I do not identify with the label *alcoholic*. Maybe that's why I never went to AA—I was not comfortable getting up in a room full of people and saying, "Hi, I'm Lisa, and I'm an alcoholic," when I did not believe it.

I use the terms *alcohol-free* and *sober* (and occasionally *teetotaler*, which is making a comeback). I don't say that I'm in recovery or have alcohol use disorder, but I do concede that I was partly dependent on the substance and the lifestyle.

If I had to embrace any label, it would be "gray area drinker"—a designation that is gaining acceptance. Jolene Park, a functional nutritionist specializing in gray area drinking, describes it as "the space between the extremes of rock bottom and every-now-and-again drinking ... which can negatively impact lives."

I wasn't an every-day drinker, and I didn't feel as if my life was falling apart. In fact, many gray area drinkers are crushing it at work, at home, and in other areas. Once a gray area drinker sends alcohol packing, though, it can cause them to reevaluate career and life paths that once seemed preordained.

My Unfurling is not a traditional recovery story. Nor is it a self-help manual. While I pass on some of the strategies and resources that helped me get unstuck, I do not purport to know what will work for others.

As it turns out, alcohol was just one of the strands keeping me bound. Once I quit drinking, it was my job to find and unwind the other strands.

So, let's start at the beginning.

One

SEEDS OF DISCONTENT

Mom, Part I

At nine years old, my mother had one of her kidneys removed, just months after having an emergency appendectomy. I can only imagine how terrifying this must have been for my mom—and for my grandparents to have their young child go through such a major operation. This was in 1948, and the doctors said that with one kidney, my mom probably wouldn't live much past her forties.

During her lengthy hospital stay, young Debra learned how to use her medical condition to manipulate people. One moment she would be up trying to help the nurses and acting all sweet, then as soon as her mother came to visit, the nine-year-old would hop back in her hospital bed and turn into a demanding brat (in my mom's own words).

One physician told my grandparents that they should take Debra and move out to the shore for an indefinite convalescence. Though they did not follow this suggestion, I believe my grandparents did end up handling their daughter like a fragile doll.

I should pause here to note that my mother has lived into her eighties, and over the past decade I've discovered that she has a creative memory. Her mind seems to possess a filter that records memories differently from how the events occurred. I can't detect a pattern: sometimes the filter makes the experiences more pleasant; sometimes it makes them less pleasant. And it doesn't happen all the time. My mom actually has a darn good memory for someone her age, especially when she *wants* to pay attention. (She never fails to notice when I have a new purse or pair of shoes.)

When I realized that my mom was recalling major life events differently from how they happened, I felt as if the air had been sucked out of me. How much of my own inception was misremembered? Could I trust any story she'd ever told me?

I came to terms with the situation because I did not want to go on in a state of constant distrust. For my mother, the stories she tells me are real. They are her truth, and they impacted her actions accordingly. For my own peace of mind, I made the decision to believe her words unless I had solid evidence to the contrary.

Back to young Debra ...

My mother shared with me that when my grandparents first got married, my grandfather told my grandmother that they could have kids as long as *she* took on the duty of raising them. I guess this was a perfectly reasonable thing for a man to say back in the 1930s. My grandmother accepted the deal, and my two uncles were born a couple of years apart. She acted as their primary guardian and disciplinarian.

According to my mom, my grandfather held up his end of the bargain and was mostly hands-off with my uncles. Then along came my mom, and my grandfather could not resist his baby girl.

Now, I love my uncles dearly, but I assert that as boys, they resented their little sister's close relationship with their dad, and this contributed to their persistent teasing of little Debra.

After she came to live with me ten years ago, my mom opened

up about a lot of stuff. She confessed that in her teens she started thinking she might be "mentally retarded" because everyone was always doing things for her. One time when she was in her early twenties, she was visiting with family friends. They were preparing dinner and requested that she make the salad.

She asked, "You trust me with the salad?"

They responded, "Of course, we do!"

That evening helped my mother begin to see herself differently, yet she continued to feel deficient. I witnessed my uncles teasing her well into their senior years. My mother's "ditziness" was part of the family lore, and it appears to have functioned as a heavy weight on her shoulders.

Recently, she remarked to me and her friend Ruth: "When God was handing out brains, I thought he said something else, so I hid behind the door!"

My heart ached for her. To me, this did not sound like a joke my mom had made up on her own; it sounded more like a mocking comment that had been directed *at* her when she was young, one that she learned to repeat.

Getting pregnant at the age of twenty-five without being married added to the family view of Debra as a screw-up. My religious grandparents were ashamed. Mom says they told her that they couldn't hold their heads up at church. They sent Debra away to stay with a friend overseas during her most visibly pregnant months. They even urged her to give up the baby for adoption at birth. Instead, my mother held her ground and kept me. It was both brave and selfish.

Brave because in 1965, being a single mom by choice was uncommon. Brave because she knew she was being judged as a flagrant sinner. Brave because when my mother told my father that she was pregnant, he refused to accept any responsibility.

But why selfish? Well, I submit that my mother longed for a baby who would be dependent on her, a child to give her life meaning. She was insecure, and motherhood might elevate her status.

And while being a mother did fill her with purpose, it also led Debra to question herself. Had she made the right decision? Was she a good mother? Would her daughter have been better off with another family?

These questions haunted both of us for far too long.

My mother and I lived with my grandparents for most of my childhood, and they never made me feel unwanted. There was a lot of love in our family and a lot of judgment, too. The fate of my eternal soul rested on my ability to be a good girl.

Inside our little house, my mom and I formed a tight bond. When I was little, she would put me to bed and sing me to sleep with a whole roster of songs, including "If I Knew You Were Comin' I'd've Baked a Cake," "How Much Is That Doggie in the Window?" and "I Found a Million-Dollar Baby (in a Five-and-Ten-Cent Store)."

She often did something called "pat, rub, scratch" on my back (which is exactly what it sounds like) to help me nod off. When *she* was getting ready for a nap, I might sneak into her room and we would take turns tracing letters and words on each other's backs as a guessing game.

From an early age, I sensed a darkness in my mother. Because my father had been given the chance to be in our lives and opted out, indignation simmered underneath her sadness. Small setbacks frazzled her, and she was quick to anger. I worried about her and wanted to make her happy. As best I could tell, my mom's day-to-day emotional stability teetered on my conduct.

At the same time, a shadow was growing in me as well. I became frightened that I would develop a terminal illness. In the 1970s, cancer was a hot topic. In the TV movie *Death Be Not*

Proud, which aired when I was ten years old, heartthrob Robby Benson (who appeared in the pages of my teen idol magazines) portrayed a seventeen-year-old boy with a brain tumor. Burned in my memory is a scene where Benson walks down a long aisle to get his high school diploma. His head is wrapped in a large white bandage that covers a protruding growth on his head. He lumbers slowly down the aisle with glazed eyes. The scene is supposed to be inspiring, but I was horrified. If this could happen to someone so young, it could happen to me.

I started biting my nails and tapping my teeth, which drained some of my nervous energy, and I liked taking refuge in the closet when I was feeling anxious. I developed superstitious behaviors. For example, if I accidentally dragged one foot on the ground while I was walking, I had to drag the other foot for the same amount of time to even things out. If I dragged the second foot too long, I would try to make up the difference with the first foot, and so on.

I don't remember ever talking to my mother about how unsteady and fearful I felt. Maybe if I had, I would have learned much earlier that my mother and I both shared obsessive-compulsive tendencies, including a penchant for reliving past mistakes and anticipating future calamities.

It's unlikely that young Lisa and Debra would have been able to articulate their mutual need to know that everything was going to be okay and that they were worthy people. Instead, the single mother and the only child put expectations on each other that neither was prepared to fully satisfy.

Fatherless

A t first, my family led me to assume that my mom and dad had been married and that he had left when I was too young to remember him. I was only about six or seven when they cleared up the story, informing me that my mother and father were never wed. His rejection of my mother became a central part of my origin story—the first man who didn't want me.

The details of what happened were filled in for me over the years. My mom met my father when he was visiting the office where she worked as a telephone operator in the 1960s. Decades later, Mom and I would watch the show *Mad Men* together, and she confirmed that the show got a lot right about how men and women interacted in the workplace during that time.

At an office where my mom worked when she was in her early twenties, one of the bigwigs offered to set her up in an apartment as his mistress. At the company where she met my dad in 1964, her boss literally chased her around his desk. She told this story to my father during their brief relationship, and he threw it in her face when she revealed that she was pregnant. Maybe her *boss* had knocked her up, he suggested!

There were no DNA tests in the 1960s, and a lawyer discouraged my mother from taking this man to court for child support. And so, my dad had effectively relieved himself of all obligation.

Before I was old enough to grasp that not having a father made me different from the other kids, his absence wasn't that big of a deal. Or, rather, I didn't sense how much it mattered. But it did.

My mother spent most of her young adulthood living with her parents and her child, with no partner in the house to be her ally. I could not comprehend her loneliness, even as it permeated our lives.

It played out in the way that she always seemed so tired, in the way that she couldn't work up the energy to do something she had said she would do. I was often hurt and let down.

If there had been a father or a peer in the household for my mom to lean on, the pressure on me to be my mother's reason for living would not have been so great.

I use the phrase "reason for living" not as an exaggeration. When I was still a kid, I learned about a letter in my grandmother's chest of drawers that my mother had written in an emotional meltdown, in which she explained how her baby was the only thing keeping her going. I remember finding that letter when I was around ten years old and reading it, my hands shaking. The gravity of my mission as my mother's daughter was coming to light.

When I look back at photos of my mother from before I came along, I see that she was beautiful. At one of the weddings my mom attended while in her early twenties, the photographer followed her around the whole time. In a picture taken at that wedding, my mom stands next to the bride and groom, and she is stunning with her teased blonde bouffant hairdo and curve-hugging dress.

The mother I knew didn't look like that. She told me that pregnancy had ruined her figure, and she had been cursed with teeth that went downhill fast. As I entered my teens, I wanted my mom to expend more effort on her appearance, to wear makeup and color her hair. If only she worked a little harder at it, I speculated to myself, she could snag a man.

Maybe what she needed more than a significant other was appropriate mental health care. Spurred by a major episode of depression, Mom finally got some counseling through the church, though it didn't last very long. Highly competent, intensive long-term therapy could have helped her considerably. But who's to say that that would have resolved her self-doubt and hypersensitivity?

My mother had a series of close women friends who modeled for me the value of female friendship. I loved spending time with my mom and her friends, like Marilyn, the hairstylist and small business owner; Brenda, the nurse; and Trish, the dietician. Mom was so much more relaxed when another adult was around who wasn't one of her parents.

In my early teens, the unfairness of this situation started to crystallize in my mind. Why didn't I have a father? Why did I have to be my mother's emotional support?

Also, I couldn't help wonder what this man with whom I share half my genes looked like. Did we share any features? What did he sound like? Would we get along if we met?

For years, I wove fantasies about finding him and winning him over, or making him feel guilty, or getting revenge—or some combination thereof.

Well into my thirties, I continued to make up scenarios. One was like a Lifetime movie, where I would track him down at his big fancy office and storm into the conference room in the middle of an important meeting, slamming my hand down on the table and announcing, "I am your daughter, and I'm going to take control of this company!"

Another was an idea for an HBO series about a woman very much like me who decides to find her dad because she is considering having a child and wants to know more about her medical history. She becomes embroiled in the drama of *his* family, which includes two half-sisters to my character (in real life, I'm pretty sure I have half-siblings out there somewhere). There's another movie concept where my dad is very ill. He uses a detective to find me, and I have to decide if I want to meet him before he dies.

With the advent of computers and the internet, I could search for him online, but my searches always came up empty. After hitting a number of dead ends, I gave up.

However, I liked to indulge my melodramatic side from time to time, to keep the feelings of martyrdom fresh. I had grown attached to how being fatherless made me unique and somewhat pitiable.

As I dug through my old journals and notebooks, I found a page I wrote when I was in my late thirties, still processing this injustice:

Doctor's Appointment

I was born with a broken heart.

Isn't that a country song?

She had a punctured heart, pierced by rejection and indifference.

Her search started early—a journey for Band-Aids and twine and caulk and whatever would do.

An incomplete heart cries out for … for what? A replacement won't do.

"The damage is done," the doctor says. "You must patch it yourself," he says.

"Fuck you," she says. "Can't you see the holes, the tears, the frayed edges? Where's my miracle operation?"

"There is no magic here," the doctor warns.

"This birth defect is not my fault."

"It's never anyone's fault."

"I would ask for *his* heart, but it's clearly compromised as well."

"So, will you choose to heal or to wallow?"

"I'm so tired of climbing in and curling up in the holes. How do I stop?"

"You just do. You'll live. It's not life-threatening."

At some point the wallowing stopped. I grew tired of it and what it said about me.

Months, sometimes years, go by without any thoughts of my father. He is likely dead by now, and I will probably never meet him. And that is that.

The pain echoed in other ways throughout my life. My drinking, my stubborn arguing, my fear of death—I dug my claws into all of them, terrified to let go.

Grandparents

My grandfather had a massive stroke when I was only three years old, so I don't really remember him from before then. My mother tells me that he adored me and that being able to communicate with me was a driving force in his work toward recovery. Mom says the first time I spoke with him on the phone after his stroke, while he was at the rehabilitation facility, I turned to her and said, "Pop-Pop is talking like a baby." She tells this story with a catch in her voice as if it happened yesterday.

Grandpop did not regain much of his speech or mobility. He mostly sat in his recliner and watched TV. If people were talking in the living room while he was trying to watch a show, he would make a big to-do of putting a cupped hand behind one of his ears—basically telling us to shut up. When someone would come over for a visit, he wanted to shake their hand to demonstrate his grip, which *was* pretty strong in his left hand.

He loved me, and I loved him. I can picture his straw hat with the green visor, the brown boxes of his Pine Bros. cough drops scattered throughout the house, and his plaid short-sleeved button-down shirts. Around the age of twelve, I went through a phase of wearing those shirts over top of my own long-sleeved turtlenecks. I loved how they looked, even if I was swimming in them.

When my grandfather's health started to deteriorate, my family made the difficult decision to move him to a nursing home. He was in and out of several facilities. As a kid, I hated those places. They smelled funny, and the people living there all seemed so lost and sad. I didn't want to visit there, but I also didn't want to abandon my grandfather in such a place.

Just before he passed away, Grandpop was in the emergency room and asked to see me. I was about thirteen at the time. I went in and held his hand, and he told me he was going home. When I came out and reported this to Mom and Grandmom, they became worried that he thought we were going to take him back to the house. I knew what he was talking about —he was telling me he was ready to go home to heaven.

The night before the funeral, my family held a viewing. I could not bear to see my grandfather's body in a casket. My mom let me stay home during the viewing. The next day I did go to the funeral. I wasn't grief-stricken, because I knew Grandpop had lived for a long time after his stroke, and he really couldn't go on much longer in his condition. Honestly, I had been preparing to say goodbye to him for years.

My grandmother was more like a second parent to me. She was smart and kind and tough. Prior to my grandfather's stroke, she worked outside the home. Mom tells me that she did something involving computers (in the 1960s!) and kicked butt at it. She often trained the young guys and then watched them rise up. Reluctantly, she retired because of my grandfather's condition and to run the household while my mom went to work.

Grandmom was our family's chief cook. She made an amazing macaroni salad. Whenever there was a big container of it in the fridge, I would grab a spoon and sneak countless bites right from the bowl. Our cupboards were full of empty margarine (we called it "oleo") and Cool Whip tubs that my grandmother cleaned out and used like Tupperware. I have fond memories of sitting at the dining table, which was in view of our tiny kitchen, tearing up bread for Grandmom's Thanksgiving stuffing. In my twenties, once I was cooking for myself, I made sure to get both her stuffing and carrot relish recipes. She didn't have them written down, so she talked me through them over the phone. I never could replicate the deliciousness of her stuffing, but I make her carrot relish every year at the holidays, and it tastes just the way I remember.

My grandmother read all the Agatha Christie mysteries, so I started reading them at a pretty early age. Although we already had an old *Encyclopedia Britannica* set sitting on our bookshelves, Grandmom bought us a new set of *World Book* encyclopedias that were more appropriate for a kid.

We used to play Scrabble and Rummy 500 in the evenings. Afterward, I would lie on the couch with my head in Grandmom's lap and she would play with my hair—one of my all-time favorite things in the world.

Most of my memories of my grandmother are good, but she was no pushover. My mom and I got into one of our screaming matches when I was no more than nine or ten, and Mom stormed out of the house and took off in her car, as she was known to do. Grandmom turned to me and said, "See what you did."

My grandmother lived to see her nineties, and we were all lucky to have had her in our lives for so long. Her mind was totally there right up until the end. As her body was failing, I went to visit her in the hospital and brought a stack of old photos of Grandmom and Grandpop and their friends. She was able to tell me who everyone was and how they were all connected.

After her funeral, we went back to the hotel room where

my uncles and their families were staying. One uncle had rented a VCR so he could show us the videos he had been shooting of my grandmother. There she was, small and mighty, telling all the old family stories of her two boys and her little girl.

As I write this, I am flooded with a feeling of love and comfort. Grandmom helped make me the resilient, curious, principled person I am today. Perhaps my father did me a huge favor by allowing my grandmother to fill the position he didn't want.

Religion

When you walked in the front door of our house, you were greeted by a large framed portrait of Jesus Christ. In the picture, Jesus had short hair, a nicely trimmed goatee, and soulful eyes. I glimpsed that image multiple times a day while I was growing up. As a kid, I was embarrassed that it hung there facing the entryway for all to see, and yet I felt drawn to it. I liked that it was different from the other depictions of Jesus that I had encountered. He looked like a real person rather than *the Son of God*.

Religion was the first and final word in our household—it brought structure, restraint, and righteousness to our family. Prior to our move to Florida, my grandparents were both deacons in their church. They were devoted to their god and the scriptures of the Christian Bible. They raised their children to worship and serve the Lord and to carry on that tradition through their own children.

There were many things we did not do in my family, including smoke cigarettes, drink (not even a champagne toast at weddings), curse (including words such as *darn*), have sex outside marriage (Mom sure messed that one up!), or waver from our faith. I got the message very early on that I needed to be obedient so I wouldn't burn in hell.

I was sent away to a church-affiliated sleepaway camp when I was about ten years old. It was nothing like the summer camp movies full of crazy hijinks and horny counselors, like *Meatballs* and *Little Darlings*. I don't remember swimming or kayaking in a lake or taking part in fun competitions—maybe because I was sick to my stomach most of the time. At night we attended lengthy worship services in a big hall where kids were asked to come up to the front to be healed from sin. The whole experience freaked me out; my mom had to come get me early.

It was around this time that I started thinking for myself. Suddenly my family and my religion were not infallible. I was finding that religion presented me with more questions than answers. We were attending a Methodist church, and I had friends who were Catholic and other denominations. The rules of various religions were similar but different. Some families drank wine and beer and didn't think it was a sin.

This didn't make sense to me. Which set of rules determined who went to heaven—our rules or theirs? What about people who didn't practice religion? Where did they go when they died? Could God tell if someone wasn't truly sorry and was only asking to be forgiven for their transgressions because they wanted to avoid hell?

I was also confused by the concept of free will versus "God's plan." I did not see why people prayed for help or guidance from God if he already had a plan for our lives. (I'm using "he" for God because that's the image I grew up with—an old man in the sky.) Did prayer really work? In the cases where prayer didn't work and someone died, such as a child, why was that part of God's plan? Why did some people suffer much more than others? Was God testing us, or was he playing with us like chess pieces?

I asked some of these questions to one of my uncles when I

was in my teens. He had attended seminary and had been a practicing pastor, so he had answers for all my questions. His explanations didn't comfort me; I was still troubled by what I saw as the contradictions within religious laws.

I thought that God was about love and understanding and forgiveness. My family informed me that this was not always the case, that God was judgmental and wrathful as well.

Once I left home for good, at twenty-one, religion held little appeal to me. I didn't care much for the philosophical tenets, and I had begun to suspect that religion functioned primarily to construct meaning in a random, scary world.

I felt that organized religion worked best as a way for people to form supportive communities—giving them a sense of belonging and purpose. But couldn't humans treat each other kindly and respectfully without stories of heaven and hell or crucifixion and resurrection?

I was about thirty when my grandmother passed away in the mid-1990s. It was an emotional time for the whole family, as she was the sun around which all of us revolved. At Grand-mom's funeral, I was crying in that heaving way that feels as if it might never stop. One of my cousins took this opportunity to remind all of us that if we didn't accept Jesus Christ as our Lord and Savior, we would not get to see Grandmom in heaven. This was exactly the kind of emotional blackmail I thought I had escaped.

Despite my resistance, the religious doctrines that my family followed became like a language embedded in my brain, impossible to fully erase.

To this day, when I fly somewhere, I pray before the plane takes off—one of the rare times that I do so. I start by thanking a god that I'm not sure I even believe in for all the wonderful things in my life, and I apologize for not being more grateful for these gifts. I then request forgiveness for all the times that I have been selfish, thoughtless, or unkind to other people. I promise to do better. Then I ask whatever supreme being might be listening to forgive me for my sins and to take me to heaven if I die. Lastly, I implore this higher power to help the plane take off, fly, and land safely.

I realize how ridiculous this might sound, for many reasons, including the fact that I'm more likely to die in a car accident than in a plane crash, and yet I don't pray before I get in a car. Of course, I wouldn't be the only person to have hypocritical beliefs and actions around religion.

A big part of my inability to fully let go of my Christian upbringing is its connection to my grandparents. My love for them will forever be linked with religion. And the imprint is profound.

Mom, Part II

My mom didn't attend college or receive any professional training, other than to learn how to operate a telephone switchboard, which was soon obsolete. During my childhood, she worked as a receptionist at a large medical clinic, as a salesperson at a department store, and on the register at a large hardware chain.

We didn't have much money, so in the summers of my tween years we might take a vacation by going to a hotel that was forty-five minutes away, near some kind of second- or third-tier Florida attraction. We would stay at the hotel and swim in the pool, and usually my mom would get a wicked sunburn within a day or two and then spend the rest of the week lying in the dark, cool hotel room while I hung out at the pool by myself.

Mom and I visited model homes together, admiring the fancy furniture, plush carpeting, and shiny new appliances. She took me and my friends to the mall and the movies, to theme parks and water parks. And she charged up her cards to make sure I had all the toys and clothes that I wanted.

When I was fifteen, about two years after my grandfather died, my mom lost her job and had what many people referred to in 1980 as a "nervous breakdown." She fell into a serious depression. Most of my memories of what happened during that time are tucked away deep in my mind.

I do recall taking a peanut butter and jelly sandwich to my mom's lightless bedroom, where she had cloistered herself. Seeing her that way made my guts churn. I didn't understand if her depression was like a virus that might run its course or more like a cancer that would only get worse. Or had she willingly retreated from our family and the world? Was I not enough to rouse her from her bed?

My grandmother eventually called her pastor, and he helped get my mom functioning and gainfully employed again.

When I was applying for financial aid for college, the time frame they used for my family's financials was the year that my mom was unemployed. I was ashamed. Again, questions swirled in my mind about whether or not she had chosen to indulge her fragility.

By the time I left for college in the fall of 1983, my mom seemed much better. And I was ready for a reprieve from feeling accountable for her moods. College was freeing for me, so much so that when I came back home for the summer after freshman year, I was agitated and out of sorts—I couldn't sleep at night, and I spent hours driving to and from my college boyfriend's house whenever my mom's car was available. I didn't even care that our Pontiac Phoenix was acting up and we didn't have the money to get it fixed. I drove around with a couple of gallon-sized jugs full of water, and if the car started to overheat (which it often did), I would pull over, wait for it to cool down, add some water, and then be on my way.

The following summer, I went away with my friend Robin to live in a beach town for a couple months and then did the same thing with another friend the next summer. I even worked as a waitress in a bowling alley rather than go home. Each summer, I didn't return until late August, when it was time to pack up for college again. I'm sure my mom could feel me pulling away and was unhappy about it, but I had grown weary of being the attentive daughter.

Within weeks of graduating from college, I eagerly moved a thousand miles away to New York City. I felt a little bad leaving my mom behind, but I saw no other way to become my own person than to put lots of physical distance between us. I did visit her over the next decade, usually once or twice a year, but I made sure that throughout my twenties my first obligation was to myself.

During this period, my mom and I visited an honorary aunt of mine. The three of us went to the mall so I could buy some new skirts for work. I was talking pleasantly with my aunt and asking her opinion on my clothing choices. She's a very nice person, and we didn't see her very often, so I wanted to make the most of our time together. Mom got jealous, and as soon as we were alone together, she told me she was worried I liked my aunt more than I liked her. I assured my mom that this was not the case, but confrontations like this one did not make me want to see her more often.

While I was living in New York, my mother worked at a day-care center and as a live-in nanny. She loved working with young children, but with jobs like these and her dependence on credit, she could not get ahead financially.

As a young adult, I became convinced that I was lacking in the appropriate amount of ambition and drive, and I blamed it on my mom for failing to set a better example career-wise. I would read profiles of celebrities and notice that their parents were often creative types themselves, or teachers, or entrepreneurs. Why couldn't I have had a successful role model for a parent? Then, I would feel terrible for asking such a question. What an ingrate I was after all she'd done for me! This is the same mom who took my first "book" that I wrote at age eleven and made copies for her friends at work. She *did* encourage my writing.

Yup, my feelings toward my mom were guaranteed to mess with my mind, as they still do.

~

When my grandmother died in 1996, my mom was at loose ends, so she came to stay with me and my first husband for what I hoped would be no longer than two weeks.

Greg and I had met at work in New York and moved to Maryland after our fast-forward romance led to a hasty city hall wedding. No, I wasn't pregnant. But I was almost thirty when we married, and there was a part of me that didn't want to end up alone like my mom. He was a catch, too—a nice, stable guy who made me *want* to be ready for marriage, even if I wasn't.

On her way up to our place, Mom got lost on the Capital Beltway that surrounds Washington, DC, and drove around in circles for who knows how long. By the time she got to us, she was like a cartoon character whose head was about to explode. It was my job to absorb that frustration and frenzy. Just like it was Greg's job to do the same when I would get all worked up about something.

Greg and I were renting a two-story house that was huge compared to our prior apartment. But with one bathroom and two small bedrooms, it was definitely cramped with my mom under the roof. She was doing laundry all the time, washing the sheets and towels way more than we did. I complained about this to someone at work, and then one day Mom came to see my office, and that coworker said, "Oh, you're the mom who's been doing all the laundry!" The fact that I had complained about Mom's behavior did not go over well with her.

I think my mother had been hoping to seamlessly transition this visit into a permanent residence. A slick feeling of dread began flowing through my veins. Wasn't thirty-one way too young to have your mother move in with you?

As fall progressed, Mom started complaining about the weather growing cold. I don't know for sure if she could tell how I felt about her being there and so she used the weather as an excuse to leave, or if she really did want to head back south.

I'm not proud of my utter relief that my mother moved on. That said, it would not have been pretty for either of us had we lived together at that point in our lives.

Mom went down to South Carolina to live with one of her nieces. My mother lived with this niece and her family for years. And though I've given them a hard time for teasing her, both of my uncles took in my mom for extended stays at various junctures in her life.

Once she was settled in down there, I took a much-needed break from my mom. I didn't call her for several months. When she broke down and called me one evening, I could hear the pain and anger in her voice.

As she told me how distressed she was, Mom brought up something I hadn't heard in a while: She proposed that if she had given me up for adoption as my grandparents wanted and I'd grown up in another home, perhaps that family would have raised me better and I would have loved them more than I apparently loved her.

It was like a slap in the face to be told that I had turned out so uncaring that my mom was still considering, three decades later, whether she had made the right decision to keep me. I could have said, *You know what, fuck you. Fuck you for even suggesting that. If you think I'm such a bad daughter, then maybe you should have given me away.* And then I could have written her off and been free, unburdened. As if.

Unsurprisingly, I chose the dutiful daughter road. As bruised as I felt, I didn't want to make my mom's anguish worse. And I knew I couldn't live with the guilt of rejecting her. So, I apologized and told her I thought she made the right decision and that she was a good mother. I explained that once in a while I needed time to myself, time to figure out who I was separate from her.

When I was going through my old writing, I found a page I had written about our relationship when I was in my late twenties or early thirties. When I read it, it spooked me a bit.

A Life Unexamined Is Not …?

A mother who starts this life. Why? The effect she has on this life. Her decisions. A girl is born. A crutch? A savior? A burden? The girl grows up, responsible. Is she now the reason for the mother's life? The support system?

A bond is formed. A strange, symbiotic relationship.

First the daughter, resentful of her mother's activities. No, Mom can't smoke; it's not right. No, Mom can't go out with a man; he might take her away. Fights, arguments, yelling, tears, jealousy, guilt.

Then the daughter grows. Fueled by her mother's own independence and selfishness, she takes on this role. Now the jealousy switches. Now the daughter smokes, she drinks, she goes off on her own to find herself and her dreams and in the process leaves the mother. Mom misses her and is hurt when the daughter can't find the time to be her partner. More guilt, more fights, more tears, more running away from problems that have built up for too long now.

The daughter has moved on to different ways of thinking, to a completely different view on life, one much more radical than the step the mother took. The other is left behind, feeling inferior, betrayed. Who are they now? How do they relate? How do they accept each other? Like past lovers, it's hard to form a trust, a new relationship, a friendship that is more honest, easy, not so bound up in need, in desperation, in dependence and expectance. Where they can tell each other everything but expect nothing.

I wrote that at least twenty-five years ago, and except for the silly part about me being so "radical," I could have written it today (I kinda did, in these very pages).

Mom and I muddled on, making the best of a relationship that would always sit atop layers and layers of resentment, remorse, and contention. We found a way to be together, to talk and enjoy each other's company. But the weak spots were never that far below the surface. The whole thing was always waiting to tumble down.

Mom, Part III

A t a cousin's wedding in 2003, when I was about thirty-eight, my mom made a point of telling me that one of her coworkers talked to her daughter *every day* on the phone. Egad! It took me a couple of years, but I relented and started calling her on Sunday nights—once a week would have to be sufficient. During one of our calls, she informed me that her kidney doctor had told her she would need to go on dialysis soon and that she did not want to do it. "So, what are you going to do? Let yourself die?" I asked.

I scheduled a visit to South Carolina so I could accompany Mom on several different doctors' appointments. Her kidney doctor told us that my mother would *eventually* need to go on dialysis, but according to her current blood work, this would not happen anytime soon. This was my first encounter with Mom's distorted memory. I did discover, however, that my mother had not been exaggerating when she told me her primary care physician often kept her waiting upward of two hours beyond her appointment time, causing her blood pressure to skyrocket. I practically had to physically restrain her to keep her from walking out.

A few years later, I caught another glimpse into my mom's

faulty memory. She was bragging to someone that I had won a full scholarship to college. I was aghast. A patchwork of grants, scholarships, and loans had paid my tuition. For more than a decade after graduating, I struggled to pay off my student loans, one of which was sent to collections. I got angry calls from a collector and had to borrow money from my friend Kelly to pay them off. And here was my mom thinking that it had all been paid for! I could feel the throbbing at the base of my skull—something that happens when my own blood pressure rises. Her naiveté was an insult. I corrected her on the spot, not caring if it humiliated her. How could she be so wrong about something so important concerning her daughter?

I don't relish dragging my mother's tender ego out into the spotlight. She is a good person at heart with many admirable qualities—such as her love of people and her initial instinct to trust that they are worth knowing.

While my mom was still living in South Carolina, I attended a work conference not far from her. After the conference ended, I met Mom and members of our extended family for dinner at a restaurant. The way my mom engaged with our server and the other people working in the restaurant was touching—she was interested in them, and the way she interacted with them had a spark of life to it. The rest of my family was quiet and almost unaware of the other people around them. It made me sad to think that some of the people at the table had looked down on my mom at points in her life (maybe still did). I felt protective of her and immediately hoped that I would carry on her openness, vitality, and inclination to reach out to people.

～

In 2009, Mom told me on one of our calls that she had just gone through a depressive period. She was living in a small studio apartment in a building that was part of a sprawling Christian retirement village. My uncle and aunt lived in a duplex a couple of blocks over, and they had helped my mom get her place there. She had not left her apartment for several weeks, and no friends or family had checked on her. I went down again to visit and discovered that she had dozens of plastic grocery bags filled with dirty clothes, sheets, and blankets stuffed in the large closet by her front door.

She did not like washing her clothes in the tiny laundry room in her apartment building. There were some senior "mean girls" who took residents' clothes out of the washer or dryer if the residents didn't get back to them in time. So, Mom had been stockpiling her dirty clothes, buying new items, and hand-washing what she could keep up with in the bathtub. I spent the week taking a portion of her stockpile to the laundromat to pay by the pound to have comforters and other large items washed, and then doing the rest in the on-site laundry room myself, where I did indeed witness the mean gals guarding their territory.

It was time. My second husband, Aaron, and I decided to move my mother up to Maryland. My first marriage had ended after six years, and I was fortunate enough to meet a super sweet guy two years later. It was another case of instant chemistry, but Aaron and I held off on saying "I do" until the initial excitement wore off and we knew we were in it for the long haul.

Now I was forty-five, and this was it—Aaron and I were about to start cohabitating with my mom indefinitely. My eleven-year-old stepson asked: "Is she going to live with you until she *dies*?"

Our original intention was to find Mom a place in a senior living facility not too far from our home. We couldn't find a place that was within her (and ultimately our) financial means, so she came to live with us.

Since then, I've realized that this was the best outcome. No matter where my mom lives, she needs a lot of attention at this stage in her life, and the idea of my driving every day to wherever she might be living does not sound any more acceptable than her sharing our home.

Our first order of business when my mom arrived was to round up a full roster of doctors for every body part and organ system she possesses. I started going with her to each appointment, taking detailed notes in a blue notebook.

We are like a traveling comedy team visiting doctors' offices all over town. She plays a combination of the jester and the contrary child, and I play the humorless enforcer who wants her to take things more seriously. I am not fond of my assigned part, but I play it all the same.

In the eleven years that she has lived with us, my mom has had both knees replaced and later fell and broke a hip, both of which involved major surgery and extensive rehabilitation; she had her remaining teeth pulled so that she could get dentures; she's had laser surgery in both eyes; and she got seriously ill from C. *diff.*, which led to a lengthy hospital stay. She is now on dialysis, and I take her to treatments three times a week.

Her doctors are constantly tweaking her sizable complement of medications, and I fill her twenty-eight-slot pill holder every Saturday night. She's had countless tests, scans, and biopsies, plus regular ultrasounds and procedures on the dialysis graft in her arm. Lately she's been having a bleeding problem after dialysis, which is not for the squeamish.

If Mom visits family for a week, that involves scheduling her to have dialysis at a center in their town and then checking in with her multiple times a day. Aaron and I used to go away for long weekends now and then, which required that we arrange for someone to take my mom to and from dialysis for a day or two. Now that she is eighty-two and the deterioration of her mobility has accelerated, we are at the point where I am no longer comfortable leaving her alone in our house for even one night.

In addition to her ongoing medical care, my mom also needs a lot of comforting and validation. I know that these emotional needs are just as real as the physical ones, and at the same time I want her to rein them in.

My mom gets this tone in her voice that is like the center of a Venn diagram if the three circles consisted of forced geniality, disappointment, and contempt. This tone was so normal to me growing up that I didn't consciously register it until I heard it coming out of my own mouth—particularly when speaking to my stepson.

The tone implies, *You have let me down, and I know you can do better.* This tone can be conveyed in a simple, "Good morning, Lisa," when I am late to check in with my mother. I realize now how much I disliked this tone as a kid and how much I hate carrying it forward. Stamping it out is very much a work in progress for me.

Part of that work includes uncovering the thoughts that lurk behind the tone. For me, it typically means that I am feeling unheard or disrespected. My mind is telling me that it's because I really am a loser—and employing this tone is a misguided attempt to assert control.

My mother expresses her insecurity in less cryptic ways as well. A lot of her joking, off-the-cuff remarks involve people being mad at her, not loving her, or begrudgingly spending time with her. She has a sarcastic, self-deprecating bit about how specific people (usually men) "cry" when she goes away because they're going to miss her *so much.*

Then there's the time we were on a road trip and stopped to use a public restroom. A woman close to my mother's age was brushing her hair, and as she stepped away from the mirror, my mom said, "You look beautiful." The woman laughed at the unexpected compliment and said thank you.

If the scene had ended there, it would have been a nice moment between two senior women. But as the other woman turned to exit, my mom added, "Now you're supposed to say the same to me." *Jeez, Louise.*

In the summer of 2015, my friend Robin and her boyfriend came for their annual visit, which that year happened to fall on my mom's birthday. Aaron and I gave my mom cards in the morning, and I'm certain the gifts she had requested were presented before our guests arrived.

That night we made an elaborate dinner for everyone, and my mom ate with us. Aaron and I then went out with our friends to watch fireworks on the lake in our neighborhood. Gliding across the dark water in our kayaks, we felt it was the perfect night.

When we got home, my mom had left a note in the kitchen passive-aggressively shaming me for not baking or buying her a birthday cake. It said something like, "If there was a birthday cake, I could take a piece next-door to Ruth tomorrow."

I ended the night choking back tears in the bathroom as I brushed my teeth.

I had helped Mom consolidate her out-of-control credit card debt before she moved up, but within a couple of years she had resumed spending money she didn't have. The term *retail therapy* was created for people like my mom, and I've been known to use shopping to fill a void, too.

In early 2017, my mom came home after going out to lunch with Ruth, and she confessed that they had stopped at a furniture store after lunch and that she had opened a line of credit to purchase a new mattress (which she didn't need). After numerous calls and arguments with the manager to get the purchase canceled, I decided to find my mom a therapist. Was I being a little punishing? Maybe.

Dr. Ryan was a great fit for my mother, and he liked me to

join them for a few minutes at the end of her appointments. One day, I took a deep breath and unloaded:

"Has my mom told you that well into my adulthood she continued to question her decision to keep me? And that she said this to me when I was about thirty?"

Dr. Ryan looked to my mom for confirmation, and she nodded her head.

I went on, trying not to cry. "That was really painful for me. The implication was that I would have grown up to be a nicer and more loving person if someone else had raised me. I guess I'd just like to know that she's gotten past that doubt."

My mom responded, "Yes, I'm over it. I think I have a pretty amazing daughter."

As much as that should have put the issue to rest, writing about it now produces the same raw feelings that made me want to yell at her on the phone that long-ago evening.

Though our relationship has mellowed, we still clash over her endless demands and my desire to "fix" her.

Recently, I went down to say good night to my mother. She was sitting on her bed, without her dentures, and she appeared small and vulnerable—nothing like the woman who used to tower over little me and whom I scrambled to keep up with when we were walking. She looked up at me, grabbed my hand, and asked, "Am I too much trouble?"

Gulp. I told her she wasn't. But in all honesty, I still feel as if I can never do enough. That night, I would have loved for her to say, *Lisa, I know how much you do for me, and I'm going to make an effort not to ask so much of you.* Instead, once again *I* reassured *her* that all was well.

This might sound awful, but here goes: I have fantasized about being able to press pause on my mom so that my husband and I might go away for a whole week without having to worry about her. I feel queasy contemplating what this says about me.

The unwanted intrusion on my life is not the sole reason I

have this thought. I genuinely do care about my mom. I don't want her to feel alone or scared. I don't want her to have a fall with no one else in the house. She fell once while I was at work, dropping and breaking a couple of glass bowls in the process. Luckily, she wasn't injured, and she had her cell phone in her pocket, so she was able to call me. Afraid that she might cut herself, I told her not to move. I drove home from work, my heart pounding, thinking about her sitting there surrounded by broken glass. What if something like this (or worse) were to happen while Aaron and I were hundreds of miles away?

This endless sense of responsibility can be overwhelming at times. My mother and I are intricately tied to each other, and I feel compelled to step in and fill the cracks where she is fractured. To put it bluntly, I don't think my mom ever fully grew up. From a young age, I felt more like her parent than her daughter, and that feeling only intensifies as the years pass and my mom becomes less self-sufficient. I am honored to be able to help her now that she's in her eighties; but for a very long time, I yearned for a less complicated, less needy mother.

As it turns out, the interviews we did for *My Unfurling* brought us closer together and made me infinitely more compassionate toward my mother. The search for the seeds of my self-doubt also uncovered my love for her and my appreciation for the sacrifices she made.

Persona: The Cool Chick

One of the themes that emerged as I wrote *My Unfurling* was my longing to be someone else. Not a different person entirely—more like a heavily upgraded version of myself. If only I were *fill in the blank*, life would be a breeze, a blast, a dazzling adventure! These fantasies were heavily influenced by my obsession with TV, movies, and celebrities.

I envied the people who seemed so naturally suited to the roles I coveted. I loved dressing up for Halloween, but in everyday life I wasn't much good at slipping on masks or costumes.

And yet, I kept obsessing about the traits, looks, and auras that I thought would bring me happiness.

For this book, I decided to take a look at my attraction to these personas, ending each section with a peek into one or two of them. Let's start with the one that calls to me the most —the cool chick.

What do you think of when you hear the word *cool* ascribed to a person? I picture a photo from the Fairview High School 1977

yearbook. Four sophomores are posed using an open six-foot ladder as a prop. One boy sits casually atop the ladder, while the others stand next to or on the ladder. All four are wearing the style of the day—high-waisted bell-bottom slacks and button-down shirts with large collars. They look as if they have much better things to do but they've stopped to pose with this ladder because destiny demanded that their coolness be documented.

I was eleven years old when this yearbook was produced. If you compare my own photo to those of the other sixth graders, you will see that I'm one of the smallest kids in my class. Because of the unplanned nature of the schools in our community, students in grades six through ten attended our brand-new high school that year. It was a weird kind of torture for a late bloomer like me to walk the halls with these tenth graders who looked like *grown-ups*.

If I could go back in time right now, I'm sure I would see that they were just fifteen-year-olds. Heck, the group photo was taken for the student government page, so they probably weren't even the edgiest kids around. Yet they are forever burned in my mind as impossibly mature and confident.

This image sprang to mind when I sat down to write about my desire to be cool and how it has impacted my life. Soon, other images and memories started gushing forth.

That same school year, 1976–1977, ABC's *Happy Days* was the number one show on television and a favorite of mine. The character known as the Fonz, played by Henry Winkler, was a portrait of coolness. He wore a leather jacket, rode a motorcycle, was smooth with the ladies, and had an air of independence.

During my high school and college years, many of us worshipped cool celebrities such as Joan Jett, Blondie, David Bowie, Prince, Jodie Foster, Mickey Rourke, and Lisa Bonet. What made them so magnetic, beyond their obvious talents? Was it their rough edges? their sense of self? their sexual energy?

When I was a high school senior, the movie *Flashdance* was released and became a smash hit. My friends and I saw it in the theater multiple times, played the album repeatedly, and started to regret having given up dance lessons years earlier.

The lead character, played enchantingly by Jennifer Beals, checks off pretty much every coolness box. Alex works as a welder—a gritty and highly unconventional job for a young woman—and comes from "the wrong side of the tracks," a common signifier of a cool character in movies and TV.

Alex moonlights as an exotic dancer in a bar and is very comfortable with her sexuality. She is extremely talented and doesn't want to accept favors from her rich boyfriend to help her get ahead. The character dresses in a distinctive way that actually set fashion trends out in the real world. Many young women and girls, myself included, followed her lead and cut the necks out of our sweatshirts so they would hang off one shoulder.

I wanted to be like Alex—self-assured, sexy, gifted, and principled. Oh, to be that fit, that beautiful, and that self-possessed.

The screenwriter of *Flashdance* advanced a rumor about how Beals secured the part. He claimed that the head of Paramount asked a bunch of macho crewmen on the studio lot to tell him which of the three women finalists they most wanted to fuck. As crass and sexist as this might sound, the rumor plays into the allure of the character, and made me want to be like Alex/Beals even more.

I should acknowledge here that coolness is a perception, and my idea of who is cool might not be the same as yours. While being seen as cool normally comes with admiration and accolades, it isn't necessarily a trait that guarantees a happy or long life.

When I made a list of famous people whom I consider cool, I noticed that many of them—James Dean, Billie Holiday, Jimi Hendrix, Janis Joplin, Gia Carangi, Keith Haring, Amy Winehouse, Anthony Bourdain—died too soon. Apparently, a not uncommon downside of coolness is a correlation with a short, turbulent life.

I also observed that cool people frequently come from blue-collar, sometimes troubled, backgrounds. Perhaps a hard-scrabble early life produces a potent blend of competency, grit, and defiance. But cool people can emerge from all economic classes. In fact, I had a relationship in college with a cool chick from a well-off family—more on that later.

Thirty years after *Flashdance* hit the big screen, I read the novel *Gone Girl*, and it struck me how well author Gillian Flynn understood the desperate need of women like me to come across as cool in their interactions with men. As I turned the pages, I was horrified to see my inner thoughts reflected back at me by the book's unstable main character. That fear of being an uptight nag, a pathetically insecure woman—there it was, captured perfectly on the page.

When I sat down to write *My Unfurling*, I opened up a folder on my laptop and my eyes landed on a document from several years earlier titled "Hi Evie." What the heck was this?

I opened the file and *ugh*! It was a letter to an author with whom I had established a teeny-tiny level of contact through Facebook. Evie (not her real name) had accepted my friend request because we had a mutual friend. She was very engaging online, and it felt as if one *could* be friends with her in real life.

By my estimation, Evie is an official cool person, and the comments on her posts suggest that others agree. She is a kick-ass writer, wears cool band T-shirts, once had an important job at a famous tech firm, and by her own admission leads an unconventional romantic life.

Here are a few lines from my letter to her along with my current reactions (please keep in mind that I was 52 years old when I drafted this):

You are a very talented writer, a fierce woman, and an all-around interesting human being. [*Gag.*]

I have been following the buildup to the release of your book for a little over a year now. It has been so vicariously exciting! I would say that I'm proud of you, but that would sound weird coming from someone who barely knows you. [*Oh, Lisa.*]

I'm sure you've heard this a million times by now, but as I read your book, I was startled over and over by how much we have in common. [*You don't say!*]

Luckily, I did not continue writing much past that line and thus never sent the letter.

I am positive that each and every human—no matter how we dress or wear our hair or what accomplishments we might have—worries about their cool quotient at some point. And for me, at least, crushing on the cool kids is alive and well, even in middle age.

Two

SELF-DOUBT TAKES ROOT

First Grade

When I was about five years old, my family moved to Florida because the doctor had recommended the warm weather for my grandfather after his stroke. Fairview was originally supposed to be a small retirement community. However, not long after the first houses were built, a nonstop flow of families with young kids moved there from New York, New Jersey, Connecticut, Pennsylvania, Ohio, and so on.

In first grade, I had to travel on the bus to the next town over to go to elementary school. Kids of all ages would crowd onto the bus and take an hour-long ride (counting all the stops) to the neighboring town.

The younger kids were dropped off first, and then the high school kids. One morning, I looked up and saw the bus pulling into the high school. I had been lost in my thoughts and had failed to get off at the elementary school. I was sitting next to a teenager who had not noticed that a tiny little kid was still next to him.

I was terrified and embarrassed. All the kids around me were so big. I was taken to the principal's office, and he called the elementary school to let them know I was there. Then the principal drove me in his car over to my school. As a shy six-year-old, I found it very unnatural to be in an unfamiliar car with a strange adult man. I was going to be late to class, and all the kids were going to look at me and laugh. I must have been crying, though I don't recall the feeling of tears running down my face. Just my heart beating fast and my stomach in knots with anticipation. What happened when I arrived at the elementary school is not in my memory, but the whole event was traumatic enough that it is forever lodged in my nervous system.

That first grade year kept delivering experiences that would stay with me for a lifetime. Starting at a pretty young age, I would get bouts of stomach cramps and diarrhea and would have to spend long periods in our bathroom at home. At school, the bathrooms closest to my classroom were fully enclosed small rooms, each with a toilet and a sink. There was a small square window at the top of each door—too high for a child to peek in yet high enough for an adult to check on the occupant.

One day, I was lingering on the toilet, maybe because of cramps or maybe because I was lost in thought again. Suddenly our teacher's face appeared in the high window— she was glaring at me to indicate that I was taking too long. She was a grouchy teacher, and seeing her face scared me nearly to death. After that event, I stopped going to the bathroom at school. Because of the long bus ride on either end, this meant I was refusing to pee for eight or more hours each day. My teacher must have figured this out and word got back to my family. I was sent to see a child psychologist, who according to my mom reported that I was very bright and not to worry about me.

I have no idea if that's precisely what the psychologist said, and the resolution of the issue is unclear. Did they force me to take bathroom breaks? Was the teacher instructed not to check on me if I took too long? I can't say for sure. I do know that the image of her face with her furrowed brow and huge eyes, as if she had caught me doing something vile or sinful, is one of the scariest things I've ever seen. Later in the school year, that same teacher got in trouble for putting masking tape over our mouths when she thought the class was too noisy!

Our class picture from that year is among my vast collection of photos. It is faded and crumpled and tells a story. As in many class photos, the kids in the back row are standing; the kids in the middle row are seated; and the kids in the front row are kneeling on the floor. That scary teacher looms in the back looking disheveled and a little unhinged. The real kicker is me: For some reason they were short one chair for the middle row, so I was forced to share a seat with another girl. I'll call her Zelda.

Share is a very kind word for what's happening in the photo. Zelda has her shoulders squared and displays the comfortable posture of someone who is sitting on *her* chair. Zelda has apparently given me a couple of inches of the seat (or did I have to forcibly take it?). I am smiling and leaning into Zelda to keep from falling on the floor.

This photo makes me mad to this day. Why didn't our teacher or the photographer scare up another chair for me? It was a school, for God's sake—there should have been chairs everywhere! Was I so small and unremarkable that they didn't think it mattered that I didn't have my own seat? Why couldn't Zelda have scooted her dang bum over a couple of inches more? Did she resent having to share her chair with such a little runt?

Looking at this photo is an exercise in rewriting my story. I can choose to be angry on behalf of little Lisa and cling to feelings of invisibility and disgrace, or I can see a girl who smiled despite her circumstances and went on to learn how to claim her own space in life.

Best Friends, Part I

M y friend Robin entered my life when we were eight years old. I can still trace the exact path to her house in my mind, and I remember her family's phone number. I recall the layout of her home, the plush shag carpet, and the screened-in swimming pool out back.

Robin was extroverted and energetic, and we shared many loves, including acting out weird stories with our dolls. A couple of years in a row we held used-toy sales in front of her house to make money for Christmas gifts, and we turned a tidy profit. We bonded over our appreciation of food, movies, TV, and all things pop culture, and we could talk for hours about anything and everything.

The two of us met Julia at age nine, when her family moved into a house on the next street over from mine. Julia was fun and charismatic. I found myself doing things I might not normally do when I was with her. There was something irrepressible and original about her. Maybe it was because her dad was a professional clown and Julia used to work parties with him as his sidekick, Dimples.

Robin and Julia were both "high-spirited," as one might have said back in the 1970s, and I was drawn to their energy.

We rode our bikes around the neighborhood, played tennis, listened to music, and took dance lessons together.

When Robin and Julia teamed up, anything could happen. I was a tad envious of their chemistry. The two of them played a prank on me at one point, calling me several times on the phone, posing as the "mad phone caller." I even received a letter in the mail from said caller. I wasn't so much scared as I felt like the butt of a joke. As I was writing this chapter, I asked Robin if she remembered playing such a prank; she didn't, though she added that it was absolutely possible she and Julia had done this to me.

Now, I could write an entire book about the good times I've had with my close friends. But that's not what *My Unfurling* is about. So, some less than flattering details are going to be spilled onto these pages.

The people pleaser in me is nervous about telling some of these stories. Having been raised to manage my mom's emotions, I imagined it was my responsibility to make sure everyone in my circle got along and that no one was mad at me. I was steeped in the fragility of my mother, and that sense of uncertainty transferred to my friendships and, later, my romantic relationships.

Okay, back to business …

While I made a few other friends during grade school, none stuck quite like Robin and Julia. They were the sisters I had longed for.

What I didn't want to be, though, was their *little* sister. We were supposed to be equals. To many kids and adults, my small size and shyness made me almost invisible, and my curly hair made me an oddity. I also carried a doll around for way too long, marking myself as shamefully immature. I'm fairly sure I was still carrying that doll when I started developing my first crushes on boys!

When we were about eleven or twelve, Robin, Julia, and I were at the grocery store and a woman asked them how old I was. I was standing right there, and this woman looked over and past me to speak with my older-looking friends. Who knows why this lady gave a crap? When people weren't ignoring me, they were busy caring that I didn't fit into some agreed-upon template for an adolescent girl.

Being behind physically meant finding myself forced into time-out at random moments. In sixth grade, the girls in my class were passing around the seminal Judy Blume book *Are You There, God? It's Me, Margaret.* I asked one of the girls what the book was about, and she told me I wouldn't get it. The funny thing is, the book is about a girl who is anxious about going through puberty—and I could totally relate to that. Plus, my mom had told me about all that stuff already. When I did read the book, I was pretty pissed off that these girls thought they knew more than me just because their bodies were developing faster than mine.

In elementary school a group of girls started the BOP Club (the acronym stood for "Boys Over-Powered," though I don't think this was a radical alliance). Robin was part of the club from the start, and the next year Julia was invited thanks to some zealous lobbying from another friend of hers.

The members of the club came to school in matching customized T-shirts that they had bought at the mall. The local paper ran a photo of some of the girls standing at a table outside a store, having a bake sale for charity. During the three or so years of the club's existence, I was never a member. I had heard that they might finally ask me to join, but then the club dissolved. It had run its course, and some of the girls were growing apart. The queen bee girls who led the BOP Club no longer ruled our class.

I wonder what inspired a group of young girls to form an exclusive club. How *did* ten-year-old girls become popular, anyway? Being outgoing and confident and having similarly charming friends mattered. Being pretty and having nice clothes also helped. And having parents who socialized with each other surely counted for something.

When we were about twelve, my friends and I took dance classes together at a studio that was a half-hour's drive from where we lived. A carpool was organized so that the moms could take turns driving us to and from class each week. One of the moms did not want my mother to be part of the carpool. I don't know what her objection was, but there were inklings.

Was it because my mom was the only divorced woman in the group? Maybe because my mom and I lived with my grandparents and we were of a lower economic class than the other families? Or was my mom considered reckless and untrustworthy? I think all these things were tied up together without people realizing it.

All I know is that every week for about a year, I would arrive at the dance studio alone, having been driven by my mom, while the other girls arrived together. This ridiculous arrangement eventually collapsed, and Mom and I were permitted to join the carpool. I'm guessing one of the other mothers stood up for mine (and for common sense)—possibly Robin's mom, who was outspoken and practical.

This injustice had gotten under my skin. A subtle hum developed inside my core, alerting me that there was something different, seemingly inferior, about me and my family. No one I knew (or their mothers) invented the practice of including and excluding others. We were all unwittingly caught in an age-old story that pits people against each other based on their differences. Intentional or not, this exclusion made an impact on me.

While I was in my awkward phase, Shannon moved to town. She was small and young-looking and could relate to my exasperation at being a late bloomer. We were both smart and funny and quickly formed a bond. For a few years, we were glorious dorks together. While all the other girls were watching *General Hospital* after school, Shannon and I were obsessed with *Guiding Light*, writing numerous poems and spoofs about the characters on the show.

As I was going through my own writing, I unearthed a folder full of the artwork and jokes that Shannon and I would pass back and forth in class.

Shannon would sketch a boy she named Junior, who was always getting into trouble and calling on his mom to come rescue him. During our early high school years, I would beg her to draw new Juniors for me, and his plights grew more elaborate over time. In return, I would draw my character Super Bubble for her—the joke being that I was not capable of sketching anything more intricate than a circle with crude arms and legs and a cape.

We ended up becoming high school cheerleaders along with Julia. We left those dorky little girls behind. But we never forgot. Well into our twenties, after a few drinks, Shannon and I would recollect how miserable it had been to lag so far behind all the other girls.

We both majored in creative writing at college. Shannon was a Hemingway gal, and I was Team Fitzgerald. We read and reread Ann Beattie's *Chilly Scenes of Winter*, Lorrie Moore's *Anagrams*, Margaret Atwood's *The Edible Woman*, and Laurie Colwin's *Home Cooking*.

We were serious Lynda Barry fangirls and often recited from her comic strips. We also devoured *Bloom County*, *FoxTrot*, and Matt Groening's (pre-*Simpsons*) *Life in Hell* cartoons.

Out of nowhere, one of us might say, "Cat, hat," and together we would finish: "In French, chat, chapeau. In Spanish, he's el gato in a sombrero." I have no idea how or when this started. It's from a song in the 1971 *Cat in the Hat* TV special, and we kept it up for decades.

That dorky girl still lives inside of me, and she forgives me for being in such a rush to ditch her.

School

S chool was a constant source of whiplash. I was bright and well-behaved, so teachers adored me. And I welcomed their praise. I liked getting good grades, I loved to read, and I was discovering a passion for writing.

At the same time, I was tiny and timid, so my peers looked down on me. The cool kids saw me primarily as someone they could cheat off of on tests. And forget about gym class—I was always one of the last kids chosen for a team.

I pored through old yearbooks as part of my research, and in my sixth and seventh grade books, virtually every class-mate's signature refers to my size. Here's a sampling:

"You might be little but I still think you are nice. Stay little and cute."

"You're a sweet & nice little [underlined twice] girl. Good luck in the future."

"Hope you get taller! Have a swinging summer!"

"I'm glad we were good friends this year. I hope we will still be friends next year. Have a nice summer. And please try to grow a couple inches!"

"To a real nice girl and I hope you have good luck on your growth in the future."

"A girl with a big heart, but a little body. Good luck in the future."

"It's been nice knowing you this year. Hope to get to know ya better next year. Good luck in all you do—especially with the guys. Don't worry you'll grow."

"Have a nice summer, good luck with the guys, and stay short, you look cute."

That last one sort of underscores what it felt like. That signature was from one of the prettiest girls in class. It was nice of her to say I was cute, but I didn't want to be cute. I hated the way these kids saw me.

Even my own best friends liked teasing me. There was a period when I said a couple of dumb things in close succession, and they awarded me the nickname "Dense." I had come to expect being teased for my size. But being targeted for a malfunctioning brain really stung. My intelligence was the one thing I clung to when times got tough. Having it challenged made me question whether my smarts were the life preserver I presumed them to be.

One of my supposed dense episodes involved my mistaking a Porsche for a VW. When I was growing up, our German next-door neighbor had a Volkswagen Karmann Ghia. I saw that car parked outside his house every day for years. When I was about ten years old, my friends and I were packed into a car being driven by one of our parents, and a familiar-looking car passed us.

"Look, a VW!" I exclaimed.

My friends all cracked up. "That's a *Porsche*, Lisa!"

I was humiliated. I also didn't get it, because it looked so much like the VW that sat next to our house.

This bothered me enough that about five years ago, I finally decided to do some googling, and I learned that the two cars were, in fact, related. I won't bore you with auto design details. Trust me, though, I read enough to feel thoroughly vindicated. I share this little story because it demonstrates how long I could nurse the pain associated with my friends laughing at my stupidity.

In my mind, I wasn't allowed to mess up even once. It was too risky to my shaky sense of self.

Once when I was in sixth grade, my friends were all out of school on the same day, and I had to figure out what to do at lunch. I didn't want to sit alone, so I went up to a table with some girls who were friendly with my friends and asked if I could eat with them. I was holding my lunch tray, arms trembling, and the mouthiest girl at the table told me no. I don't remember where I went to eat—I just remember absorbing the toxic notion that I wasn't good enough for them. Outside my small circle, I carried no weight.

In my tween years, I had a series of imaginary friends who helped me feel better about my standing in the school hierarchy. I would talk to them in my head, and they were always there for me. I felt normal with them. Bridget was my companion for a year or so, and then there was Deandra. In time, my writing took over as a way for me to create characters and situations that validated my feelings and demonstrated that some kids had it worse.

In reality, I didn't need to create stories to see that other kids were in pain. In our school, there were a few kids who were viciously teased and ostracized. These were kids who came from poor families, kids who were heavy, and kids with body odor issues or bad acne. I would never compare my life to theirs, but I could relate to their predicament. Witnessing how these kids were treated made my stomach ache, though I'm sure at times I went along with the names we called them.

One family had three kids close in age—the boy was in my class, and his two sisters were a little older. I remember a particular bus ride home when one of the girls was trying to sit down, but none of the kids would share a seat with her. She was trying to push her way onto a seat, and the boy sitting there used his body to knock her down onto the floor of the bus. The look on her face as she stood up was one of pure hatred. I didn't know what to do. I was about twelve years old and looked much younger. Who would listen to me if I were to say something? I wish I had stood up for these kids. No doubt I was intent on clawing my own way up to being treated with respect.

Despite feeling like a pariah, I was drawn to participating in extracurriculars. I liked trying new things to see what I might be good at and keeping myself busy.

I acted in school plays, which amazes me. I have a terrible singing voice (I swear, this is not my inner critic speaking), and yet I auditioned for chorus three years in a row until the music teacher gave up and let me in. I competed in the science fair, making it to the county level with a project in which I tested the product claims made in a variety of TV commercials. I briefly joined the Future Business Leaders of America and attended a competition in which my subject was Economics (too funny).

And then there was cheerleading—that ultimate look-at-me activity—which I started in ninth grade. How did the little girl with the big pouf of frizzy hair ever summon the guts to try out?

Doing these things—performing in front of other kids, competing, being evaluated, listening for the differing levels of applause when each cheerleader introduced herself at pep rallies—only served to crank up the anxiety I felt most of the day. I was afraid of failing, of being laughed at, of looking like a fool for even trying.

I'm impressed that young Lisa decided she had the right to stretch, to strive, and to put herself "out there" in a school full of kids who had little interest or faith in her.

Body Image

When I was in first grade, someone from a local newspaper came to our school and took photos of the kids at recess. In a picture that ran in the paper, a girl and I are playing catch. We were at the respective far ends of the size spectrum for our age, so she appears to be huge while I am tiny. I'm sure the editor loved the contrast and that's why the photo made the paper. Instead of being excited about being in the paper, I felt shame that my smallness was on display.

Two of my own photos from childhood stand out. One is from a dance recital when I was about ten years old. I am posing with two other girls backstage. It's hard to tell my age because if you were to see me alone, you might think I was six. Posing on either side of me are two girls from my class who tower over me. It's kind of creepy how small and doll-like I look in my jaunty tap dance costume. The second photo is from a year or two later at a dance convention my friends and I attended at Disney World. The ballroom is packed with girls in pink tights, leg warmers, and leotards. I am looking at the camera, and my face is gaunt, my body so much smaller than those of the girls around me.

On the bus ride home from school, when I was about

eleven or twelve, Robin and Julia were teasing me about my size. They were brainstorming what was the smallest thing they could call me, and they came up with *embryo*. They found it hilarious, but it filled me with disgust for them and myself. I hated being so different, being an object of ridicule.

My class photos over the years start out cute, and then I get stuck for a long time. In my eighth grade photo, my hair is a fuzzy cloud around my head, and I'm slumped over, practically receding into the bottom right corner of the photo.

Around that time, a boy sitting at the desk behind me in class took his hands and lifted up my layers of curly hair, crying out, "Set them free!" I was sure he was implying that bugs were trapped in my hair. It made me feel like a freak.

All the while, I was buying *Seventeen*, *Mademoiselle*, *Glamour*, and other fashion magazines. Phoebe Cates and Whitney Houston were two of my favorite teen models before they became famous. *Vogue* covers featuring the top models of the early 1980s, such as Kim Alexis, Brooke Shields, Kelly LeBrock, and Kelly Emberg, were taped to the walls in my room. A poster of Jaclyn Smith from *Charlie's Angels* hung over my bed. I would stare at these women, who were all paid to be gorgeous, and ponder why I couldn't be willowy and beautiful.

In the late 1970s, I was dancing around my living room to the soundtracks from *Grease* and *Saturday Night Fever*. I yearned to be able to sing and dance like Olivia Newton John and to look the way she looked in those black spandex pants at the end of *Grease*. As a kid, I saw that movie five or more times (back when you *had* to go to the theater), and I don't think it ever registered to me that Sandy completely changed her appearance and pretended to smoke in order to win over Danny. I was fixated on how sexy and beautiful she looked.

I wanted breasts so bad that I used to spend hours locked in my room stuffing my bra with tissues and looking in the mirror. I would take my upper arms and squeeze together what flesh I did have on my chest to create the vertical line of cleavage that I coveted.

In ninth grade I finally started my period. My class photo that year shows a girl who looks much more poised. This time, I take up all the space in the frame, and I look close to my actual age.

My small body came with a few advantages. I had moved from taking ballet and gymnastics classes at a dance studio to training at a real gym with the gymnastics equipment I had seen in the Olympics. The uneven bars were my favorite; I wasn't half bad on the beam; and the vault terrified me. I was thinking I might try out for the lowest-level team, and then … the aerobics craze took off. The owners of the gym started pushing the equipment toward the walls so that they could fit in larger and larger aerobics classes. The gymnasts could see the writing on the wall—we were no longer their top priority. Also, my breasts were starting to develop, and I was less comfortable wearing a tight leotard, so dropping gymnastics and trying out for cheerleading made sense to me.

Thanks to aerobics and Jane Fonda's toned body, the bar for female hotness had been raised. Everywhere I looked, I saw images that made me feel inferior. Girls were exercising, counting calories, and bitching about their thighs.

When those curves I had longed for arrived, I could scarcely enjoy them. Now, I had large boobs on my petite body, and I felt as if everyone was gawking at me. Not only were strangers leering and making rude comments, some of the guys we hung out with took to calling me "LBT"—which was a play on my initials and stood for "Little Big Tits."

I became obsessed with my weight, staring at myself in the mirror and fretting over how I looked in clothes. During my teen years I dabbled in dieting, fasting, and purging. I never fully took to any of these behaviors, but my mind was often swirling with thoughts of self-loathing for eating too much, not exercising enough, or having a stomach that stuck out too far. I would lie on my back at night, running my hands across my hip bones and wishing they protruded more.

When I was about sixteen or seventeen, my family was visiting one of my uncles and his family. A friend of theirs was over at the house and mentioned that he was a photographer. He and his wife offered to take photos of me at their home studio. I jumped on the opportunity because I was under the illusion that I might become a model. Love's Baby Soft (a girly perfume brand marketed to teens with slogans such as "Because innocence is sexier than you think") was often calling for fresh-faced models, and I thought I might use these pictures to enter one of their contests.

At the house, the couple showed me contact sheets of photos they had taken of other women. In a couple of the pictures, one of the women had taken down her top, and though the images were small, I could plainly see her naked breasts. I worried that they were going to ask me to do the same.

I still have the photos they took that day. The woman did my makeup, making me look way older—and not in a good way. They had me pose in front of a wrinkly blue satin backdrop, and the lighting was harsh. I brought a couple of my own outfits to wear, and they had a cheerleader's uniform on hand that I changed into for a few pics. I even wore the same strapless blue velour jumpsuit that the woman on the contact sheets was wearing. I did *not* take my top down, and thankfully the idea didn't come up.

While I was not model material, the photos document that I *was* thin and had beautiful hair. And yet, I existed in this odd culture-induced zone where it was possible to believe that I was unattractive, but also attractive enough to be a model. Needless to say, my entry to the Love's Baby Soft contest went unanswered.

〜

At college, lying out at the pool was a major activity; we scheduled our classes around peak sun time. How I looked in a bathing suit was a big deal. I wanted to look like the girls on the swim team—slim hips, long legs, flat chest.

Most students put on a few pounds in our first year, some of us the full "freshman fifteen." In early writings about my weight, I didn't examine the wisdom of this quest for physical flawlessness. I took it completely at face value. I knew that beauty accrued some serious benefits for women, and I wanted those benefits. Most of all, I wanted to feel deserving of love and attention.

In the Intensive Journal I kept for my freshman-year self-development class, I referred to myself as a "weak ball of fat." I wrote, "I could love my body, its proportions, if it was thinner," and "I'd die if guys thought I was fat or if I knew my body was unappealing."

My friends and I decided not to rush any of the sororities and instead became "little sisters" in what was the second-hardest-partying fraternity on campus. That first year, the Greek system on our campus had a big competition with lots of wacky outdoor events. This included a tan contest, which surely would have been won by a sister in our fraternity who was known for her tan. This chick and her squad were running late, and the brothers needed someone to take her place. I don't know how I let them talk me into representing our fraternity in the contest. I was not tan by most standards unless you looked at my tan lines and noted how pale I had been to start.

Each girl had to parade in front of a panel of student judges (and the audience). As I walked by, I pulled the strap to my bikini top to the side so they could see the difference in my skin tone. I'm pretty sure the judges put me through to the finals just to make me walk out again. Someone from the crowd shouted, "This isn't a titty contest!"

I guess one good thing came from this experience—I never entered any wet T-shirt contests on spring break.

In my sophomore year, I started to wake up to the external forces at work, and I gave an oral report in a health class suggesting that body image and eating disorders exist on a spectrum. I mentioned how I occasionally took fattening foods (such as my favorite Brown Sugar Cinnamon Pop-Tarts) and chewed them up to taste them, then spit out each bite into a napkin. A girl came up to me after class and thanked me for talking about this, and she and I bonded over our shared fear of being fat.

Scenes like this one played out again and again throughout my life—women sharing their body image fixations, often with an awareness that it was a game we couldn't win, and other times with enthusiastic buy-in. Knowing that the beauty and thinness racket was a con didn't make it any easier to opt out. And the propaganda was so enticing.

In 1985, the summer before my junior year of college, Jamie Lee Curtis starred as a fitness instructor in the movie *Perfect*. With her long legs, tiny waist, and full breasts, Curtis's body was like the Holy Grail. Who among us could look like that? Yet, didn't I owe it to myself to try to get as close as possible?

Around that time, I developed a love-hate relationship with the *Sports Illustrated* Swimsuit Issue, which I bought religiously throughout my late teens and twenties—years spent trying gimmicky diets and celebrating when an illness meant losing a few pounds. Fortunately, I never went to extremes to try to look like the women pictured in that magazine. But my brain sure was preoccupied with measuring my body against the ones I saw in those magazines.

From the ages of thirty through forty-eight, I worked at a feminist group, the National Organization for Women (NOW). During those years, I helped provide content for a project called the Love Your Body campaign. Toward the end of my tenure there, I put together a massive slide presentation that could be viewed online or downloaded to present to groups. I poured all my frustration with media images of women into that slideshow. Many people reached out to NOW with grateful comments, such as: "As a fifteen-year-old girl, I feel these subjects are important to acknowledge and discuss. Thank you for addressing this sabotage on our health and self-esteem."

I felt like a fraud for critiquing the very stereotypes and narratives that I was so susceptible to falling for myself. And yet, that is what made my work so resonant, the fact that it was grounded in my own anger and insecurity.

At the conclusion of the presentation, I outlined what freedom from beauty ideals can mean for girls and women, including "more time to focus on school, work, hobbies, athletics, politics, community, personal fulfillment, spirituality ... more time to build for the future and develop skills that will last."

Reading this now, I see that I just as easily could have been referring to the gift of freedom from drinking, media consumption, shopping, and other distractions.

Even in my fifties, I'm vulnerable to gazing at social media influencers and female celebrities, wishing I could look more like them. Would I have more followers if I had long flowing hair, legs for days, big eyes, and prominent cheekbones? *Look at her in that cute outfit—I will never look like that!*

As I write this section, I continue to step on the scale every morning. I want so badly to accept my body, to treasure it. A whole new set of worries haunts me as I get older—such as my graying hair, my sagging neck, age spots on my skin, and an intense fear of varicose veins. Perhaps this dissatisfaction with how I look will never go away. The conditioning is deep and relentless.

Hair Story

M y hair has a story all its own. Up until I was ten years old, my hair was very blonde and somewhere between wavy and curly. By the time I was in fifth grade, it had gotten long, and it looks very pretty in my dance photos from that year. If I had left it that way, it still would have been unique, but maybe not quite such a hassle.

Early in 1976, when I was eleven, ice-skater Dorothy Hamill won gold at the Olympics and became famous for both her talent and her shiny, swingy wedge haircut. My mom took me to a hair salon that summer, and I told the stylist I wanted my hair cut like Dorothy Hamill's. The woman did not warn me (or my mom) that the texture of my hair would look very different in a short, layered bob cut.

You can see the aftermath in my sixth grade picture: my hair is a fluffy mushroom hovering around my head. The cut made my hair curlier and thicker, and I battled against it for the next five years. I wanted to be like the other girls, and I didn't understand why I had to be different in so many ways.

I tried everything to tame my hair. In my early teens, I started getting it professionally straightened at a local salon. Even chemical straighteners couldn't make it lie perfectly flat

—there were always a couple of tenacious ridges that refused to smooth out. One time, it went right back to being curly after one shampoo. My mom dragged me back to the salon, and they performed the process again, only about a week after the initial treatment. For the next couple of weeks, my scalp hurt. In the shower, I gingerly ran my fingers through my hair, afraid it was all going to fall out. That was the end of chemical straightening for me.

After that experience, I cycled through several methods I had read about in magazines. One tactic involved taking my soaking wet hair and wrapping it around my head with a million bobby pins and then sleeping that way. It was very uncomfortable, and my hair was frequently still wet under the pins when I woke up. Next, I switched to washing and then braiding my hair into a million skinny braids and sleeping like that. This temporarily reduced the volume of my hair, and it vaguely resembled how girls with straight hair looked when they used the same braiding technique.

As I went through this wrangling, I would think about a photo someone had taken of me from a weird angle where my hair looked like a giant pyramid jutting out from my head. That photo made me feel like an ugly freak.

The real problem, as far as I was concerned, was another female celebrity and her fabulous hair. This time it was Farrah Fawcett, who exploded on the scene in fall 1976 in the TV show *Charlie's Angels*. Looking at photos now of her feathered hair, I can see that it had bounce and, dare I say, a touch of curl. The way her hairstyle was interpreted by the girls at my school, though, turned the look into rigid wings plastered against the sides of their heads. I can still see girls in class taking out their big combs and flipping back those feathers, doing this repeatedly and then patting the hair flat. I wanted to be able to do that, but my hair would not cooperate.

The closest I got were these hideous tubes of hair on the sides of my head that are on display in my tenth grade photo.

To achieve this nonalluring look, I used to blow-dry my hair and then put an old pair of stockings on my head like a tight cap for about twenty minutes to calm it down. Then I would use the curling iron and lots of hairspray to create the tubes. What effort for such an awful result!

Once my friends and I turned sixteen and started going to the beach together, I discovered that if I just let my hair dry curly, it didn't look half bad. So, by junior year of high school, I was finally wearing my hair in a style that suited me and didn't require so much work. It was so thick that I had to pull back large chunks from the sides with barrettes. This became my secret weapon, because if I was trying to get into a bar without being carded, I would take out the barrettes and let my hair go wild, which made me look older.

I never did learn to leave well enough alone when it came to my hair. Right before my friends and I went to a rock concert when we were sixteen, I applied a temporary auburn color that was supposed to look natural. The cheap product turned my hair a vivid Raggedy Ann red. These days it would look totally hip, but I was embarrassed to go to the concert like that.

Then, in college, all the male soccer players had mullet cuts, and for some bizarre reason I decided I needed to wear my hair that way. So, one night I grabbed the scissors, gathered big handfuls of hair from each side, and gave myself a mullet right there in our dorm room!

In my third year at college, I made yet another visit to a salon, this time clasping a photo of a woman with perfectly straight hair and asking for the stylist to give me her short asymmetrical cut. It was another disaster that took years to grow out. I also fried my hair with Frost & Tip home hair coloring, skipping the highlights cap and glopping the product all over my head. If this helps you picture it, my favorite writing professor used to call me Tennis Ball Head. In my first year in New York, I tried to cover this yellow color with a light brown shade, and it turned a lovely green that inspired some of my coworkers to affectionately call me Sigmund the Sea Monster, after an old children's TV series.

In my twenties, I stopped experimenting with my hair, right around the time that I became convinced I was going bald. I would use a hand mirror so I could look at the back of my head in the bathroom mirror, pulling sections aside so I could inspect my scalp. It did, indeed, get thinner as I approached middle age. Isn't that what I wanted all along— hair that was easier to manage and wasn't so big?

I am back to coloring it again in an effort to delay going gray for as long as possible, but the truce I called with my curls stuck. It's a peace I rarely pause to appreciate. I take this as a hopeful sign that I can learn to accept other aspects of myself so completely that my comfort becomes second nature.

Best Friends, Part II

When we arrived at school for ninth grade, Julia suddenly looked like a young woman. I was so jealous of how her butt looked in jeans! All the guys were noticing Julia, especially older guys, which I thought was the ultimate compliment.

Looking back at our high school photos, I see that Julia was stunningly gorgeous—long dark hair, amazing cheekbones, sparkling smile. In senior year she was named class flirt—the only one of my circle to win a class superlative. She was the first of us to embrace punk and new wave music and fashion, and her taste in guys tended to be outside the box.

Nights out with Julia were often unpredictable. One time it was just the two of us, and we went to a hotel bar that had a reputation for not carding. It was so weird to sit at a table in a hotel bar at the age of sixteen. I felt sophisticated with all that soft amber lighting and live piano music. Two guys came over to chat us up, and Julia told them we were home from college. The excitement of keeping up the lie for the next hour was both terrifying and invigorating.

At our high school graduation party at Robin's house, Julia, in all her beauty, got down on the ground and did "the worm"

—a dance move that was basically squirming around on the floor. She did this in front of Robin's older brothers, earning my eternal admiration.

As we started to mature, Robin and I ended up being attracted to some of the same boys, and they to us. My first real kiss was with Kyle Clark. A couple of years older than us, he was short, cute, sexy, and a bit of a troublemaker.

I was in tenth grade and a junior varsity cheerleader when I met Kyle. He was old enough to play on the varsity football team, but because of his size he was playing JV. We were getting ready to come back from an away game, and he kissed me by the bus. That weekend I spun around on my front lawn in pure joy. I was going to have a boyfriend! Maybe I was finally going to catch up with the other girls.

Not much later I found out that Kyle liked Robin. I wondered if I was too immature-looking and inexperienced for a guy his age. I was heartbroken and wanted to lash out. One of my friends helped me put masking tape all over his clunker of a car in revenge.

Robin went out with Kyle for at least a year, so I had to get used to their relationship. He became her first, and I admit I was a little relieved because I didn't think I was ready to have sex yet. I did make out with him again about a year later at a party, which helped stroke my ego.

Kelly moved to Fairview when we were in tenth grade. She was in our same grade and almost a full year older than us. I had no images in my mind of her as a kid—it was as if she came to us fully formed. Kelly had the appearance and demeanor of someone calmer and more adult than the rest of us, and her boyfriends were usually older. I often wished I could be more like her.

Kelly and I had some memorable adventures together. Because she had gotten her license first, she would drive us around in her yellow Chevy Vega, which she hated, but it got the job done. I couldn't believe my luck at having such a mature friend.

When we were juniors, there were several senior girls who kept threatening to kick our asses over boys we had fooled around with. Our high school held an annual "powder-puff" flag football game between the junior and senior girls. A few of us decided to join the junior team. Why did I want to be part of a girls' football game? I was terrible at team sports! Was it a foolish grasp at relevance in the high school ecosystem? If so, I came off as a wuss instead. Kelly and I sat side by side on the bench the whole game to avoid being beaten up on the field.

Robin, Julia, Shannon, and Kelly made me feel that I belonged, that I was worth spending time with. We went to rock concerts and partied together, commiserated over idiotic boys, and got in trouble for doing all kinds of absurd shit, such as putting a condom on a pickle at a diner before we left. Our server was a kid we went to school with, and he totally ratted us out.

As much as I loved my friends, I was always comparing myself to them. This one had tanner skin, this one longer legs or a smaller nose. Why couldn't my hair be more normal? Why couldn't I be a couple of inches taller?

It wasn't just about looks. I felt like the biggest flop at talking to guys and acquiring serious boyfriends. Inside my head, I was certain that I was the least confident, the wimpiest, and the most emotional. I desperately wanted something I could be good at, something I could be proud of. I didn't always make great choices in this quest.

Shoplifting

In the self-exploration workbook I kept for a college course, the "Crossroads" prompt directed me to list times in my life when I decided to go one way or the other, and then choose one of these intersections to write about. Of the fourteen crossroads I listed, I chose to concentrate on shoplifting, of all things.

I wrote: "It was in tenth grade when we started stealing food out of the ala carte line at lunch. ... It seemed harmless and fun. ... Then, on my own I began to take books. ... I felt as if I was doing something my friends couldn't do, or do as well, because I was brave and sneaky."

After years of feeling like a little kid compared to my friends, I was doing something dangerous. One of my friends started shoplifting with me; we hauled in clothes, make-up, and albums, and then later cigarettes and alcohol.

My entry continued: "This was a big step from my past goody-goody self, and it was all on my own. No pressure. I instigated it, in fact."

By college I had mostly quit. I admitted in the journal that I had stopped primarily because I was too paranoid. In senior year, my friend and I were caught at a K-Mart stealing pillow shams (pillow shams, for gosh sakes!). We had been so successful that we had gotten reckless. The security guard followed us out to the parking lot and made us come back inside. Sitting in that back room, we were positive he was going to call our parents. He did let us go, after making copies of our drivers' licenses and scaring the hell out of us. The fun was officially over.

Under the heading "The Road Not Taken," the workbook encouraged me to imagine my life if I had gone in the other direction. Decades later, I was a little surprised to read my eighteen-year-old self speculate: "I can see myself if I had never shoplifted. I would be a lot less daring, brave. I probably would have cheated less in school. I would be quieter, more in awe of my friends, less sure of myself."

I didn't sound remorseful at all—a little wistful, but mostly grateful that shoplifting was the gateway to leaving my innocent girlhood behind.

Who knows if I could have lived a more "moral" life if I hadn't started stealing things first? The other habits that followed, such as smoking, drinking, messing around with guys who had girlfriends, and other questionable actions, may have cropped up regardless. Maybe I was headed down that road no matter what.

Reading the words and phrases that pop up again and again in that journal—*second-rate, self-conscious, no personality, a fool, like dirt, stupid, eager to please*—I see a girl who was convinced she was less than other girls, including her own friends.

I didn't see many options for feeling better about myself. It was one of many signs that I was casting about, with little guidance, for ways to build my confidence.

The Price of Cool

Right when I should have been coming out of my shell and building my self-confidence in productive ways, I discovered cigarettes and alcohol, the shortcuts to everything I wanted—courage, coolness, attention, and adulthood.

At the age of sixteen, drinking quickly became a regular thing for me. Every weekend there was a party, either at one of the deserted sites around our development, with nicknames like the End or the Egg, or at one of the rented houses where recent graduates were living.

Early in our drinking careers, my friends and I didn't always finish a bottle of MD 20/20 or whatever crap we were drinking, and we needed to store it somewhere until next time. So, we stashed bottles of alcohol outside our homes so that our parents wouldn't find them.

We didn't try too hard to find inconspicuous hiding places. One spot was behind a low sign right off the road not too far from the elementary school. Whoever was driving would pull off the road, and one of us would jump out of the car and duck behind the sign to either deposit or pick up our bottles. One time we went to pick up the bottles and they had been smashed, with all the glass on the ground. We thought that was weird: Why not take the bottles? But we didn't worry too much about it—we just found a new hiding place.

It was such a relief to feel cool. My friends and I went to all the parties, and after a couple of drinks I didn't feel out of place. We would get drunk and make out with guys. Some of them were guys we liked, and some we didn't even talk to outside of the parties. My friends and I liked to hang on each other and fall down laughing, which led to a rumor that we were lesbians, which we thought was hysterical. A subsequent rumor started that I was at a party when someone called me a lesbian, so I banged ten guys to prove I wasn't. That one wasn't so funny.

A girl named Claire was still in our group when we were sixteen. She was a former BOP Club member who had originally been tight with the early popular girls. I had always been a little intimidated by her, but thanks to cheerleading, we were forming what felt like a real friendship.

We cheerleaders couldn't go to parties in our uniforms after football or basketball games, so we would change clothes in whoever's car we were using that night. Parked in the school parking lot, we would wriggle out of our skirts and into our jeans and then drive to the party. Claire and I did this one night in my car, and then the two of us headed to someone's house. A couple of other friends were going to meet us there.

As I was driving, a car followed us a little close and then came closer and closer. We got scared, so I made the next right turn that came up. The car turned right, too, and then drove onto the grass, where it picked up speed and pulled right in front of me. I stopped as quickly as I could and hit the car on the driver's side.

The driver got out, and it was Claire's older brother, whom I barely knew. He was yelling at me that I had dented his car, and I pointed out that he had pulled in front of me. He realized that he was at fault and that my car wasn't damaged, so he agreed not to report it. I don't remember what all was said, but it became clear that he had been following us for several weeks. He knew that we were drinking and going to parties.

Later, it would occur to me that Clarie's brother was likely the person who had broken our hidden bottles. And based on the timing, I suspected that he had been waiting in the school parking lot while we were getting changed in my car.

Claire's brother forced her to go home with him, and she reported back to the group that he had told her parents everything she had been doing. She was forbidden from hanging out with us anymore, and she quit cheerleading. We were worried about her, but we were dumb kids and let her slip away too easily.

In the second half of senior year, I stopped cheerleading and got a temporary job at a discount shoe store where Claire worked. They were going out of business, and they needed extra employees to do inventory. It was nice to hang out with Claire again.

After high school graduation, she and I didn't speak again until our ten-year high school reunion. Claire sat with us at our table, and it was almost as if she was part of the group again. Sadly, none of us attempted to resume contact with her after the reunion. Why didn't I reach out? guilt? cowardice? Was it too late to try to form an adult friendship? She was married with kids and seemed very different from us. Besides, I was too busy leading my madcap boozy sexy life in Manhattan (much more on that later).

Best Friends, Part III

Throughout the years, my friends and I went through phases where one or two pairs might be closer for a couple of months or longer, and then things would shift again. I always felt close with everyone and fancied that I was the glue that held us all together. Who knows if I really was the glue or if I simply liked the idea that I was.

Julia, Shannon, and I were accepted at the same college and went off to live together in what became a well-known dorm room thanks to the comings and goings of various guys. The name of our dorm was Bain, and our room number was 804. Someone wrote "804 does Bain" on the wall in the elevator, and we were kinda honored.

We had chosen a private university because it was closer to our homes, and we liked the small scale of the campus compared to the bigger schools we had visited. Because it was an expensive college, we were mingling with a lot of well-off kids. It was scary to be taking classes, hanging out at the pool, and attending parties with kids who were clearly well beyond our income brackets.

The male soccer players were like gods on our campus, and one player (who looked and sounded like Spicoli from the movie *Fast Times at Ridgemont High*) used to shout "Rock 'n' roooollllll" whenever he saw two or more of us walking toward him. As a college freshman, I thought this was funny. Many years later, it crossed my mind that this was his way of calling us lower class and trashy. It doesn't really matter what he meant, because once the alcohol was flowing, no one cared how much anyone's parents made or what brand of clothes they were wearing.

Robin and Kelly visited us on campus often. Robin was there so much, a lot of people thought she was a student. After our freshman year, Julia lived off campus for a while and then moved up north. Shannon and I stayed, both majoring in creative writing and earning bachelor's degrees in 1987.

One by one, we all moved to New York City (except Julia, who was living in upstate New York), with Robin leading the way. I was the next to move to the Big Apple, at the age of twenty-one, just weeks after graduating. Like on a sitcom, we each settled into our roles, which could be both comforting and constricting. Having friends who "got" me felt good, but sometimes this meant being pegged to a part I didn't want to continue playing. Was I only allowed to be the person they saw?

I wasn't sure who I was independent from my mom, and maybe I wasn't sure who I was separate from my friends, either.

As I looked through my old writing for *My Unfurling*, it came back to me how much my friends and I fought. We argued over guys, perceived slights, and bizarre stuff (such as, should we perpetuate the myth of Santa Claus with our future kids?). Many of our fights took place while drinking, though not all of them. We could be pretty mean to each other. Some might say it's a miracle that we all stayed connected as long as we did. We were nothing if not stubborn.

With Robin and me, it didn't matter what we were fighting about—it was all about the raw emotion, the screaming and crying. We were both under pressure and ready to explode—just add alcohol. Some of the most brutal memories I have are those moments when it seemed that we might destroy each other.

I loved these women (still do), and the thought of losing any of them as friends used to fill me with dread. Unfortunately, it did come to pass in a few cases. In some instances, we were able to rescue the friendship, or ourselves, but not always.

We all lived in NYC in our early- to mid-twenties, moving in and out of various apartments. Our place on West Forty-Third Street was the central hub for several years. It consisted of one small bedroom, one *tiny* bedroom, a largish kitchen / dining room in the middle, and no living room. A ridiculously small bathroom had been built into a corner of the kitchen, complete with a tall heating pipe on which we would burn our bums when trying to enter the shower in the winter.

During a brief period when I was unemployed, I used to make myself a cheese sandwich for breakfast and joke around with Kelly and Shannon as they got ready for work. We called this time "Sandwich with Lisa," and it involved various voices and characters that we all played. If my friends and I were good at anything, it was amusing ourselves.

I married Greg in NYC at the age of twenty-eight. By the time he and I moved to Maryland the following year, my circle was scattering beyond the big city, except for Shannon, who stayed there for nearly three decades.

We all visited each other as much as we could. Any get-together that involved more than two of us was often the scene of a big fight and/or a series of racy photos, some of which I still possess. (Thank gawd social media did not exist when we were in our teens and twenties, and even our early thirties.)

A year or two before Greg and I called it quits, Kelly, her husband, and Shannon came to our house in Maryland for Thanksgiving. I was drinking a lot, and apparently my unhappiness was like a dark cloud over the event. I woke up the next day to discover that Kelly and her husband had left without saying goodbye. Kelly could not (or did not want to—totally her right) handle my negativity and wallowing, retreating when I was at one of my lowest points.

About a year after my separation from Greg, a few of us got together at Kelly's house for Shannon's birthday. I was feeling sorry for myself, and consuming alcohol was only making it worse. At the decrepit age of thirty-five, I moaned that I would never find someone to love me again.

As I was getting ready to leave, Kelly said something about my self-pitying attitude and Shannon interjected, "That was cold, Kelly." Shannon rarely inserted herself into arguments, so the remark must have been pretty bad.

It had snowed the night before, and the ground was covered. As I was driving my rental car home, the sun was bright and bouncing off the white blanket of snow. I had to scooch forward on the seat and hold my hand like a visor over my eyes for hours, driving and whimpering—feeling sorry for myself.

The September 11 attacks happened eight months later, and we decided to call a truce. Shannon and I went to visit Kelly, and we all watched *America: A Tribute to Heroes*, a music special that aired early that December. We talked about how life was precious and short and said that we shouldn't let things get between us.

Less than a month later we had a huge fight on New Year's Eve of 2001—a night that I maintain altered our group chemistry forever. After that incident (which I'll get to later, I promise), Shannon and I remained close, but Robin and I didn't speak for months. I did not like this situation at all. I was in a new relationship with someone special, and my job was stressful. I was accustomed to processing my life with Robin, and now I felt unmoored. The fact that she could go so long without talking to me made me feel insignificant.

I initiated a personal campaign to win Robin back. (Yes, I was in my mid-thirties at the time.) I started sending her post-cards, and I finally landed on the perfect one. It was a black-and-white 5x7 photo taken in a locker-lined hallway of our high school about twenty years earlier. At the end of the school year, the yearbook staff would sell extra photos, so I think I must have bought this one along with a few cheerleading pics.

In the photo, Kyle Clark wears a football jersey with jeans. It looks as if he was walking away from the camera but then someone called his name, so he turned back right before the shutter clicked. He looks short, cute, and exactly as I remember him. I had no qualms using Kyle to win back my friend like this. He owed me.

I wrote Robin's name and address on the back of the photo, like a postcard, and mailed it off. That got her attention, and I was so relieved to be back in touch with her.

Kelly and I emailed a little bit after that New Year's Eve fight. I could sense that she saw me and Shannon as being largely to blame for the whole fiasco. Kelly was pulling away, and I wasn't sure there was anything I could do. Then, a letter came in the mail. It was typed and signed at the bottom by Kelly. The letter stated in no uncertain terms that she no longer enjoyed spending time with me—basically, I was bumming her out. The letter broke off our friendship and wished me a nice life.

I kept that piece of paper for a long time. I brought it to therapy and read it to my therapist. I would take it out and read it and lean deeply into my sorrow and anger. After months of this, my new boyfriend, Aaron (and second husband-to-be), told me I needed to get rid of that damn letter. So, I ceremoniously burned it in the kitchen sink.

Kelly and I reconnected down the road. Our repaired yet tenuous friendship reminds me of how pathetic and self-centered I can be and how assuredly *she* can cut ties.

Fifteen years later I found myself in a similar situation with

Shannon. I could no longer deal with Shannon's denial that she had a drinking problem and her refusal to seek help. I rationalize that I hung in there with Shannon way beyond what Kelly was willing to put up with from me. The truth is, Kelly and I both had had enough at certain points and chose to protect ourselves.

While Julia was fortunate enough to miss the New Year's Eve debacle, she was part of another huge clash at Shannon's apartment a decade later. I felt protective of Julia that night. For the first time, I saw the fragility behind her beauty and larger-than-life personality. We were sitting on a bench down by the East River, and I was stroking her long hair. I hope it didn't come across as weird, because I just wanted to comfort her. She hadn't been there for many of the ugly conflicts, so I wasn't sure if she was used to scrapping the way Robin and I often did when we said quite nasty things to each other.

These friends helped form who I was, and I won't ever be truly separate from their influence. I continued to form meaningful friendships in adulthood, some intense and lasting, but these women will always be my twisted sisters.

Persona: Weirdo

M isfits, freaks, dorks, nerds, goths, punks—I've long had a soft spot for the weirdos of the world. Maybe I was meant to be one and I took a wrong turn somewhere. I've had some odd-bird friends throughout my life, but I was too focused on wanting to be accepted to fully embrace those people and the fount of weirdness inside me.

As I was growing up in the late 1970s and early 1980s, I didn't see many geek girls on TV or in the movies. Most of the weirdos were boys, and their stories usually involved them swooning over the popular girls who were out of their league. Gender roles had loosened up enough that girls could be tough or sexually assertive, but they weren't supposed to slip into the realm of the peculiar.

Even Molly Ringwald's awkward character in *Sixteen Candles* was clearly on the cusp of becoming the kind of girl guys fought over. In fact, a year later in 1985's *The Breakfast Club*, Molly was already playing "the beauty." Ally Sheedy took on the part of "the recluse" in that movie, and her character was the closest thing I had observed on-screen to a female eccentric.

Singer and music video trailblazer Cyndi Lauper became

our offbeat heroine for a couple of years. Her 1983 debut album was called *She's So Unusual,* and her exuberant individuality was a nice contrast to Madonna's glamour and in-your-face sexuality.

Then Winona Ryder emerged. I first saw her in the 1986 movie *Lucas,* when she was in her early teens. She was playing the dorky girl who liked the nerdy boy who pined after the cheerleader. You could tell right away Winona had something special. Two years later she was in *Beetlejuice,* and she followed that up with *Heathers* in 1989, thus securing her place as the exemplar of the unconventional girl.

I admired that geek/goth look—straight black hair, short bangs, porcelain skin, red lips. As usual, I didn't fit the bill. And I didn't feel right trying—it would be like putting on a costume.

While I was writing *My Unfurling,* I watched a documentary about one of my all-time favorite groups, the Go-Go's. Guitarist Jane Wiedlin talked about the band's early roots in the LA punk scene. Wiedlin described how she used to dress, saying that people would often cross the street when they saw her coming. Oh, to be able to scare people off with one's fashion choices!

Living in New York City in the late 1980s and early 1990s, I would occasionally run into a bona fide punk with a huge neon spiky mohawk. These sightings would always fill me with a complicated mix of envy and disdain.

I dressed mildly funky in my late teens and early twenties, but I didn't have the guts to take it over the top. My arms were not laden with bracelets, and my hair, makeup, and clothes were just this side of respectable. My friend Robin was the one who knew how to pull out all the stops. I marveled at her fearlessness. Torn about whether or not I wanted people to look at me, I usually ended up on the unassuming end of the spectrum.

Of course, being a weirdo is about more than rejecting the

normal standards of dress and appearance. It's about living your life by your own values, not the ones fed to you by mainstream culture. It's about not caring (for the most part) what the "normies" think of you. It's about following your spirit and not being afraid to explore uncommon paths.

As I've gotten older, I've met a number of people who fall into this diverse group of nonconformists. I respect them so much. The heart of an offbeat person beats inside of me, and I might indulge her when I'm alone or with my closest friends. The part of me that craves normalcy, however, is too apprehensive to really let my freak flag fly.

Perhaps in my old age I'll lean into my full range of idiosyncrasies. In the meantime, being a weirdo is one pinch of flavor in my mostly vanilla life.

Three

AN INVASIVE HUNGER

What Guys Want

For a long time, I puzzled over what guys wanted. The problem was, I thought I could pin down the answer and then ascertain how to deliver some magic combination of these qualities and behaviors.

When I was in seventh grade, I knew that guys wanted a girl who looked like a teenager—which was not me. I missed out on the whole tween romance phase, where kids would flirt and hold hands and "go out." You'd see these pairs walking side by side down the school halls, sliding their hands into each other's back pockets.

Around that time, I had a crush on a guy named Ricky. At a poorly supervised party, a group of us were playing spin the bottle. No one ever wanted to kiss me. I spun the bottle and it landed on Ricky. I wanted to kiss him so bad. Someone dared us to kiss for ten seconds, so we leaned over and kissed while everyone shouted out the seconds. It wasn't really a kiss, more like touching lips. Kids joked that I had stolen his gum, and I liked being part of this joke, even if it wasn't true. This encounter did nothing to increase his attraction to me. Not long after that, he started going out with a cute red-haired girl who was half a foot taller than me and very outgoing—the same girl who wouldn't let me sit at her lunch table a year earlier, by the way.

Before we could drive, my friends and I went roller-skating a lot. One of our parents would drop us off at the rink and then pick us up again a couple of hours later. The rink was in another town, so it was full of guys from other schools—an assortment of *different* boys to ignore me.

I didn't want to stay home and miss out, but I hated going along and being reminded that I was a nobody. I must have been about thirteen when I was sitting with one of the girls on the side of the roller rink, and I looked down at the relative size of our legs. Hers were long and normal-sized compared to my tiny twigs. When was I going to stop looking like such a child?

I would watch as boys asked my friends to skate with them to whatever song was playing. None of the boys approached me unless someone had pressured one of them into skating with me. More than sitting on the sidelines, I hated skating with a boy who barely acknowledged me. We both couldn't wait for the song to be over.

I'm not sure why it was so hard for kids to understand that despite my size, I had the same feelings that they had. Maybe my hormones weren't quite as charged as theirs were, but I wanted to like someone and have him like me back. I had been getting crushes on boys for as long as my friends had, and suddenly *their* crushes were different, presumably more grown up, while mine were still those of a little kid.

As I got older, I continued to struggle with how to please guys. Even after I hit puberty, some of the guys I liked preferred my friends, which only added to my sense of inferiority. I had only one real boyfriend throughout my high school years, and I definitely wasn't in love with him. Having grown tired of pining after boys who were uninterested or unavailable, I tried to like this guy. Instead, I became frustrated and created a score sheet of all his weird expressions, checking off how many times he used each one as we talked on the phone.

Not long after graduating high school, I kissed a much older man who was from out of town. He was the epitome of coolness that I had come to revere: a good-looking, charming writer who lived in a big city and was brimming with confidence. Maybe it was a little weird that a thirty-year-old man wanted to spend time with a freshly minted high school graduate, though it didn't seem that way back then.

He and I met up several times before he returned home. On one occasion we hung out by the seesaws in the park not far from my house. Things didn't go much beyond kissing, perhaps because he knew I was a few months shy of eighteen. The physical part was great, but it was about so much more than that—at least to me. Here was a guy thirteen years older than me who was attentive to what I had to say. Talking with him made me feel smart and adult and sexy.

That brief moment in time marked a turning point for me in seeing myself as a woman and as an equal with my friends. He and I wrote each other a couple of letters that summer, and he even sent me a copy of a screenplay he had written. When I went off to college that fall, we lost touch, which was fine because I was about to acquire a whole lot of experience with a whole bunch of people.

I was nineteen when I realized that I liked girls too, and this meant that now I needed to figure out what girls/women wanted as well. When my first girlfriend dumped me for someone else, I was sure it was because I was inexperienced and hesitant. In general, I was kind of a disaster with women. They were always the ones to break up with me, unlike my relationships with men, where I was usually the one looking for the escape hatch.

No matter who I was with, my head was usually spinning with thoughts about *me* and my supposed deficiencies, which can make intimacy challenging, if not downright impossible.

The good news is, my friends also found sex and romance exasperating. In college we had a list of things that "real men" didn't do, and it was basically a list of all the shitty things guys had done or said to us. As in, "Real men don't tell you that you could look ten, fifteen *thousand* times better if only you lost a little weight."

In our early twenties, we had a running joke that guys didn't mind your flaws when the two of you were getting busy. As in, "He didn't care that I was immature when *my tongue was up his ass!*" (Yeah, we often went out of our way to be crude.)

My attraction to older men continued for about a decade. I fooled around with a number of older men at work, including a top-level executive who took me to his home in the suburbs. He was single and in his forties, and I was about twenty-five. We drove around in his expensive convertible, which made me feel glamorous and special.

In retrospect, I can't help but chuckle at my flings with older men. I thought they were bestowing upon me a maturity seal of approval. Being with them, I felt grown-up and sophisticated one minute, then silly and girlish the next. Most likely, these men were attracted to my youth. And it was usually my immaturity that prevented us from getting serious. The benefits we each derived from these exchanges were ephemeral, that's for sure.

As I aged, my interest started shifting to younger men. Now, I was the one who was excited to discover that being with someone younger could make you feel lighthearted and adventurous. And as the older person, I basked in my position of wisdom and authority. No wonder dudes had been lusting after younger women for eons!

For more than two decades, I fumbled through the world, hungry for proof that I was lovable and for someone to be my partner in life.

Was my search for affection and recognition related to

growing up without a father? I don't think you can draw a straight line between the two. The knowledge that I had a second biological parent who wanted nothing to do with me or my mom *did* squelch my self-confidence early on. And that insecurity, in turn, made it easier to compromise my integrity when romantic or sexual affirmation was hanging in the balance.

I had a number of relationships that I recall fondly, as well as some big-time crushes that I wished would have materialized into something more. I made tons of mistakes and embarrassed myself more times than I can count. There are a few actions that I outright regret.

At the risk of sounding corny, I finally realized that it didn't matter if a relationship temporarily made me feel desirable or worldly—it was my relationship with myself that had the potential to change everything.

High School Infatuation

As a junior in high school, I developed a huge crush on a boy who had a serious girlfriend. They were one of those couples whose names you said together. The whole school expected them to get married right after graduation.

Jake worked bagging groceries at the local supermarket. In those days, the "bag boys" would take our groceries to the car and we would tip them. I was usually with my grandmother, and she would give me the cash to hand to the guy after he loaded our bags into the trunk. Whenever we got Jake, he would make funny jokes. He reminded me of Bill Murray (who, by the way, was in his early thirties back then), and before I realized it, I was a goner.

I tried to ignore my feelings. Then he started to seem interested in me, and that was too satisfying to ignore. Around this time, my friends and I had started going out drinking. As the evening got late, we would wait in the parking lot of the grocery store for our friends who worked there to end their nighttime shifts, and then we would hang out there in our cars listening to music, drinking, and fooling around.

Jake and I started sneaking off into his car or mine to make out. A couple of times, after everyone had headed home, he drove over to my house, where I would sneak back out and slip into his front seat. He would lay his head in my lap, and I would stroke his hair. We definitely had a connection. We never had sex; in fact, I don't recall us going far at all.

Word got out that Jake and I were messing around, and his girlfriend was understandably pissed. She was the quiet type, so instead of confronting me, she got some of her senior friends to target me. These were tough girls, and they started to threaten me and Kelly, who had incurred their wrath over a different boy. Remember how Kelly and I sat out the powder puff football game? This was why.

I would like to take a moment to point out here that we were *sixteen years old*. I think it's ludicrous how kids used to pair off at that age as if they were ready to settle down for life. Cheating on your high school boyfriend or girlfriend was considered akin to cheating on a spouse. And the girls in situations like mine were usually the ones who got called sluts and blamed more than the guys. Maybe I'm just saying that to excuse my own behavior. I'm sure Jake's girlfriend was genuinely hurt and that in her own version of the story, I do not engender much sympathy.

While all this was going on, Valentine's Day was right around the corner, and the French Club was doing a fundraiser. In the cafeteria, the club had set up a table where you could order a singing telegram for a buck. Then, on February 14, someone from the French Club would pop into a classroom and sing a telegram to the object of your affection (or a friend). The recipient had to pay a quarter to find out who had sent the singing telegram to them.

I was sitting in my eleventh grade Mass Media class when a girl came in to deliver a telegram. We were sitting four kids to a table, and she came up to me at my table. She started "singing" one of the song options—the one that began by declaring that the sender did not like you, but then the song would reveal that this was a joke and that the sender *did* like you. The girl delivering my telegram changed the ending and said that the sender did, in fact, dislike me.

At the end she asked, "Do you want to know who sent this?"

"No," I said.

"Well, they already paid the twenty-five cents to tell you."

She pulled out a piece of paper full of handwritten names and started reading them. About halfway through she said, "You can read the rest," and threw the paper on the table in front of me.

Our teacher was furious. I think she sent the girl straight to the principal's office. She looked at me and asked if I wanted the restroom pass. I nodded weakly, took the pass, and fled to the nearest bathroom, where I cried, gasping for breath.

Julia was in French next period with the girl who had delivered the telegram. I guess word had gotten to the teacher because Julia witnessed him yelling at the girl in front of the class.

A couple of days later the same girl was forced to deliver a *nice* telegram to me, again in Mass Media, this time with a long list signed by my friends plus some people who had signed the other one without realizing what it was. I was touched and also mortified to be the center of attention in this unseemly way.

For the longest time, the feeling of that experience survived in my body, fresh and alive. I hated those mean girls, and I hated Jake, and I hated his girlfriend, and I hated myself.

Jake and I backed off each other, and life went on. He and his girlfriend did *not* get married (shocker). At our ten-year high school reunion, I danced with him, but I was drunk and didn't get to sufficiently appreciate the full-circleness of it. I do have a picture of us dancing, and that will have to do.

There would be plenty more romantic humiliations in my life as I sought validation through attention, love, and sex. That sixteen-year-old girl had no idea what other trouble she would cause and encounter.

Work, Part I

My first paying job was working for a catering company when I was about fourteen years old. The pay was peanuts and off the books. To this day, this might be the most taxing work I've ever done.

We were a fearsome crew of teen girls too young to work real jobs and older women in need of supplemental income. We would arrive at the compound (a collection of old trailers of various sizes) early in the morning, usually a Saturday, dressed all in white. The older women did food prep in one of the trailers, while us youngsters loaded up the van with heavy crates of dishware, silverware, large jugs of salad dressing, and a bunch of other supplies.

One of the women would drive us to the party, which might be local or up to forty-five minutes away (I swear, we drove for an hour once). The girls would sit in the back of the van, perched on plastic crates, bracing ourselves on the walls of the van as we rounded corners. When we arrived, we would unload the van into whatever on-site kitchen was awaiting us. The older women would start making the meal, and we would set up the dining hall.

The teens were responsible for serving the meal and

clearing the tables. I remember walking behind people with a gray bus pan balanced on my hip, surreptitiously leaning over to grab plates and silverware, while some Lion's Club dude gave a speech at the front of the room. We got lots of dirty looks, but staying on schedule was vital.

The grossest part was the little Styrofoam bowls of three kinds of salad dressing with plastic spoons in them that we had to put on the tables. These bowls sat on the tables all night, and we were strictly instructed to pour the contents of any bowl containing more than a spoonful or two back into its proper jug at the end of the night. For the sake of future guests, we did not follow this rule very well.

As we ran our bus pans to the back, I figured out that things moved fastest if I put aside any pride or squeamishness and just took my hand and smeared any excess food off the plates and into the large uncovered garbage can sitting in the kitchen.

If there was an open bar at the party, like at a wedding reception, it was run by a different business, so we might get to meet a male bartender who would sneak us drinks. We also took as many cigarette breaks as we could, with the older women always yelling at us to get back to work.

We did some dishwashing on-site, took out the garbage, and loaded up the van. Back at the compound, we unloaded the van, finished washing the dishes, and put everything away.

This all took somewhere in the vicinity of fourteen hours, I kid you not, for about thirty-five dollars cash. By the time someone would come to pick me up, I was bone-tired. At home, I would strip out of my clothes, which reeked of cheap French dressing, and sleep the best sleep of my life. If I needed the money, I might get up and do it all over again on Sunday.

I credit that caterer with helping me to develop a strong work ethic. I'm not sure if it's a good thing that I learned to bust my ass for little pay, but it made me feel good about myself.

~

As we were all getting our driver's licenses, Fairview was opening its first fast-food joints. We could put catering work behind us! All the high schoolers were applying at Burger King and Wendy's, and some of my friends got jobs. I couldn't get hired to save my life. I did eventually score a job at an independently owned Mexican-style fast-food place that was a half-hour drive away. Because we had only one car, I couldn't work that many shifts, but the food was pretty good, and we employees could eat all we wanted.

When I got to college, my scholarship included a work-study job. I used to sit with another student in the Admissions Office performing menial tasks such as counting brochures until one of us was called to do a tour. I loved taking a prospective student and their family around the campus. My friends and I had a pretty big dorm room for freshmen, with large windows, so I especially loved showing visitors our room. One day I got on the elevator with a kid and their family, when another resident said to me, "Wow, Lisa, you were really drunk last night!" Niiiice.

I worked a morning shift, so Julia was often still asleep when I would barge in with a family, and piles of our clothes were strewn all over the floor. But all that was forgotten when the family checked out the sweet view of the campus we had from the eighth floor.

To supplement my college work-study salary, I worked at a well-liked, nice-ish restaurant. I was a terrible server—intimidated by the customers, nervous that I was going to mess up, and incapable of opening wine bottles with the waiter-style corkscrew we were supposed to use. Once, to stop a dish of sautéed mushrooms from falling into a diner's lap, I thrust my hand into the sizzling butter. I had to immediately dash into the back and plunge my hand into a bin of ice. The customer made a big deal about a couple of grease spots on his suit, so I had to get the restaurant to pay his dry-cleaning bill. Shortly thereafter, I migrated to working the hostess stand and the takeout window, where I could do less harm.

Work reminded me of school. I was smart and hardworking, so I received praise from my supervisors. However, my anxious and wimpy nature made me fair game for the chefs, bartenders, and more experienced waitresses, who found me tiring—particularly the chick who kept having to open wine bottles for my tables when we worked the dinner shift together. It was like being that awkward little girl in grade school all over again.

Some weeks I made enough money to send a little cash home to my mom, who I was sure could use it. I was discovering the power of money and how it could fill a hole, however briefly, where self-respect was lacking.

First Girlfriend

I n my second year of college, I realized I liked women, too. Meg was two grades ahead of me. I noticed her early on in my freshman year. She was the type of person most people noticed, with long dirty-blonde hair that she flipped around, a fit body, and a great tan. Meg drove a gold sports car and lived off campus in a rented house. She whizzed around as if she were always in a hurry and had acquired the nickname Meg Hyper (it took me awhile to realize that Hyper was not actually her last name—maybe I *could* be dense at times).

Freshman year, I often saw Meg at the pool. One time she turned around from her lounge chair and asked me what time it was. My heart started pounding as I fumbled to look at my Swatch. That initial contact, which lasted for about three seconds, made me feel special. I don't think I was aware at first that I was attracted to her. I just thought it was exciting that someone so hot and older had spoken to me.

Early in my sophomore year, I started crossing paths with her more frequently on campus. Walking by, she had an energy that electrified the air around her.

Lots of people on campus went to a downtown gay club on Wednesday nights because the bar had a ridiculously cheap rail drink special. Students would go there and get drunk and then move on. My friends and I started going there, and sometimes we would dance or watch the drag show. One night, I was coming out of the restroom as Meg was going in. We sort of nodded and smiled at each other. As I headed to meet my friends on the dance floor, I felt all tingly. She had recognized me!

And although I knew there was a chance she was there for the drink special like we were, I was almost certain I had discovered that she was a lesbian. And that delighted me even more.

Things escalated from there. Meg said hi to me the next time we passed each other on campus. A week or so later I was in the microfiche room in the library when she came in, sat down next to me, and started chatting.

Out of nowhere, Meg asked, "Are you going to be at the club next Wednesday?"

"Um, I don't know," I managed to squeak out.

"I'm going to be there, so you should go," she asserted.

I felt like I might pass out. "Uh, okay, I'll try."

"See you there," Meg said with a smile and then exited the room.

Was this a date? I was officially freaking out. What was I going to do? Should I tell my friends?

The night in question, my friends and I went to the bar. They wanted to leave early, before I had time to hang out with Meg. I hadn't told them about my conversation with her, so as we drove away, I knew I had to speak up. I told them that I thought maybe I was attracted to Meg, that we had been talking on campus, and that I needed to find out how I felt. Julia agreed to go back with me to the club and we dropped the others off elsewhere.

I kissed a woman for the first time that night. And thus began a whirlwind couple of months. Meg and I hung out at her place together, where she would make us dinner and then we would go out to the club. She invited me to come visit her in South Florida over winter break. After Christmas with my family, I flew down to spend a week with Meg and her family (my family thought she was just a new friend of mine from college).

Meg's family had money. Her mom was nice but very appearance-focused—giving Meg a hard time about gaining a few pounds at college, which I found crazy, as Meg didn't seem to have an ounce of fat on her.

The Madonna album *Like a Virgin* had come out the month before, and we were listening to it obsessively. We lay out in a hammock in Meg's backyard together for hours listening to Madonna and talking. It could not have been more perfect.

The relationship did not last long. I never felt like Meg's equal; I was waiting for her to discover that I wasn't edgy, or bewitching, or lesbian enough. And we were only nineteen and twenty-one after all. Not long after school started back up in January, I could tell that Meg was losing interest. Sure enough, she moved on to a woman named Willa she had met at the bar. As I had feared, my successor was taller and prettier than me (and she had a cool name, to boot!). I was heartbroken because I did like Meg and because this confirmed my suspicion that I wasn't good enough for her.

I remember getting all weepy after seeing Meg and Willa kiss at the club one night and having to be taken care of by a good friend of Meg's whom I barely knew. Yeah, it was embarrassing. I went back to guys for a while after that, initiating a pattern that went on for years. After a woman would break my heart, I thought maybe I'd be on better emotional footing with a man. Truth be told, my fragile ego was at a disadvantage regardless of gender or orientation.

New York City

After graduating college in Florida, I lived in New York City for close to eight years—most of that time in Midtown (otherwise known as Hell's Kitchen), and about six months in Brooklyn.

The first apartment Robin and I shared was a tiny studio on West Forty-Third Street. It was a great location, and the rent was cheap. My closet was about a foot and a half wide, and the pole on which I hung my clothes was balanced precariously, so when I opened the door, the whole thing often fell down, and I had to put the pole and all my clothes back up again each time.

After a year in the studio, we moved to a two-bedroom apartment on the same block, which was a palace by comparison. Robin and I painted the walls a pale pink and redid the kitchen floor in large black and white checks (I'm sure she did most of the work). I took the smaller bedroom, and I loved the fire escape outside my window. A photo of me holding a beer out on that fire escape is one of my all-time favorite pics. I'm 22 at the time and working a good-girl-gone-seedy vibe, from my messy hair down to my short fingernails with the chipped polish.

There were restaurants on three of the corners of our block.

A large Food Emporium grocery store occupied the fourth corner, and there was a live theater on our block that ran well-reviewed plays featuring talented actors such as Kathy Bates.

We ordered food from the Greek diner on Ninth Avenue a lot. I fell in love with breakfast sandwiches from the delis and bodegas around us. We did our laundry at a noisy, crowded place until we started paying the extra money to drop it off and have it done for us.

There were numerous bars in our neighborhood, one of the hippest being Mike's, which was known for its killer margaritas and how they decorated the place in a new theme, such as *Twin Peaks*, several times a year.

One of my first days there, Robin took me to Mike's. I thought the bartender was very cute (my gaydar was not yet refined). I ordered a bottle of Bud, and he shook his head at me.

"Sorry, we don't sell Budweiser here."

I stared at him, not knowing what to say.

He took pity on me: "If that's what you're used to drinking, why don't you try a Rolling Rock? I think you'll like it."

As he slid the beer across the bar to me, I felt like an idiot. I did appreciate the recommendation, though, and went on to drink Rolling Rock for many years.

Robin and I went to foreign and independent movies down in the Village. We waited in line at a popular Italian restaurant where you could bring your own bottle of wine. We walked all over that city. I never grew tired of looking up at the tall buildings.

One by one, the rest of the group migrated to the big city (everyone except Julia, who was living upstate). We rotated in and out of that apartment in our early twenties. I was the only constant there. Eventually I had to start taking in roommates I didn't know. That's how I met Oscar when I was about twenty-five. Talk about timing. What could have been a temporary roommate situation turned into a lifelong friendship. With his biting humor and up-for-anything attitude, Oscar became an honorary member of our group, and a particularly close buddy of Shannon's as well.

One of the things I adored the most about NYC was the way you could go into a restaurant and plop yourself down at the bar, which was almost always at the front, on the right side just as you walked in. Usually, I talked to the bartender or someone else at the bar as I waited to meet a friend.

In my first year in New York, I went to one of our usual places on the corner. A woman in her sixties or seventies was at the end of the bar drinking Manhattans with a slightly shaky hand. She offered to draw a sketch of me, and I jumped at the offer. The pencil drawing she handed to me was very faint, and I loved it because she had made me look more like Madonna than myself.

Living in a city that was walkable and also full of taxis, buses, and subway trains meant that the drinking habit I had established in college could continue undeterred. Many a night I passed out in the back of a cab on my way home, and the driver would have to wake me up when we got to my place. On one occasion, I locked myself out of that first studio apartment. We were on the ground floor, and our window was a little higher than street level. I grabbed onto a cable that was attached to the building and Spider-Manned my way up to the top of the window, where I could pull it down and then climb in, falling through the blinds to the floor inside.

I could fill *My Unfurling* with nothing but crazy New York stories if I so desired. I learned to talk to strangers over those years, and the results were decidedly mixed. If you went out in the city with an open mind, you never knew what might happen. Most of the time it was good, or maybe I was damn lucky. (I did get mugged on my own block late at night my first year there, and that was pretty terrifying.)

So, I have a confession: Despite my insecurities, I knew I was good-looking—not a head-turner, but pretty enough to grow accustomed to the benefits afforded attractive women. I had drinks and dinners bought for me. I went to plays with men I considered friends who paid for my tickets. I could usually count on a guy talking to me if I went up to him in a bar. I could flirt my way out of trouble. My smile and my sufficient comfort with femininity absolutely contributed to the wild ride that was living in the big city.

Drinking, and hooking up, and a long line of relationships kept me busy. Did I have fun? Hell yes. It could also be damn lonely.

The day Kelly moved out to live with her boyfriend sucked big-time. Shannon had already moved across town months earlier, so now I was alone. I was about twenty-four, and I had long dreamed of living by myself, but not like this, not feeling abandoned. The bedroom that Kelly and Shannon had shared was dominated by a utilitarian unfinished-wood bunk bed set. The room was emptied out, and I was feeling sorry for myself. As I went to sit down on the bottom bunk, I banged the back of my head on the wooden frame of the top bunk. The pain and sadness made me yell *"Fuck!"* and burst into tears.

I lived a total of seven and a half years in New York. It felt much longer—in the best possible way. I met lots of fascinating people and some real characters you could not make up. I learned to be tougher and more self-reliant there. Anything seemed possible, and I started expecting big, awesome things from my life—not because I had seen them in movies, but because I could feel the potential for them as I walked the city streets.

First Serious Relationship

In 1988, I met my first serious boyfriend at work in NYC. I was in my early 20s, and Brian and I went out for two years—a record for me at the time. He was sweet and funny, but I'm sorry to say that I mostly remember our arguments. We used to walk together part of the way home after work. He lived on Long Island, and I lived in Midtown Manhattan, so we would part ways at a corner in Times Square. I always wanted him to come home with me, and oftentimes he couldn't (or didn't want to). So, we would squabble at the corner a couple of times a week, with me going full drama queen when the mood struck me.

How many people saw our fights? Maybe some of the same people who passed that way every evening witnessed them. I was desperate to get Brian to do what I wanted. If he didn't, then I was a failure—unlovable, not desirable, and not persuasive enough to change his mind.

Brian and I had one of the worst arguments I've ever had with someone relative to the matter at hand. We were lying in bed before going to sleep, and I had a headache, so I took two Tylenols.

"How long do you think it will take for the pills to start working?" I asked him.

"I don't know," he said.

"But if you had to estimate, how long would you say?"

"I have no idea."

"Just take a guess." (This was long before we could have looked it up on our phones.)

"I seriously have no idea."

"I don't understand why you can't just say a number—like ten minutes, twenty minutes, half an hour!"

My head was pounding, and now I was yelling and making it worse. I could feel that throbbing at the base of my skull. I started wailing, and I even banged my head against the wall a couple of times (something I've only done twice in my life). Brian got me to calm down, but he still refused to make a guess about the Tylenol.

In hindsight, I see that my propensity for anger was an outgrowth of my fear that I wasn't worth squat. In this case, I felt as if his refusal to give me the estimate I had requested was a sign that I didn't rate an answer.

My mom had issues with anger, too. When I was a kid, we would have screaming matches in the living room, and she would storm out the front door, jump in her car, and drive away—leaving me terrified that she would get into an accident because she was so worked up. Or possibly never come back. Looking at our deserted driveway, I would think to myself: *What if that was the last time my mom and I saw each other, and we were fighting?*

Consequently, I have tried not to run out on uncomfortable disagreements. This means I often dig in for too long instead.

Letting a disagreement sit there without trying to win the other person over to my side is unthinkable. Like a dog with a bone, I don't like to give up. Violence has never been a component of my temper. I don't want to hurt anyone. But I do occasionally want to smash things. In college, I discovered how gratifying it was to throw a drinking glass against the wall behind the kitchen sink and watch it break into pieces.

More than any other boyfriend or girlfriend, Brian saw this side of me a lot. I could also be a pretty crappy girlfriend. One Sunday I was supposed to go out to his family's house on Long Island, and I blew him off because it was Earth Day and I wanted to go barhopping with my friends. That's right, we weren't doing any Earth-related activities—we were day drinking, which happened to be my priority that particular Sunday.

Poor Brian. I was new to the give-and-take of committed relationships, and I was a selfish mess. He was kind to me and understanding when I wanted to break up. I'm not sure he would have been so nice if he had known that I had started fooling around with a married man. It was good that I set Brian free. He needed to meet his future wife, and I had lots more misbehaving to do.

Heartbroken

G wen and I met in the early nineties, when I was twenty-six. She was in New York City for a couple of months to participate in an immersive sales training program at the office where I worked. She was smart and pretty and had a mature confidence about her that I admired. Everyone agreed that she was going to make a great salesperson.

I started to suspect Gwen was queer. One night the sales trainees went out with the employees for drinks, and she and I started talking. We came out to each other pretty fast, and things escalated quickly given the limited period of time she would be in town.

She told me she had a girlfriend but that they were in the process of breaking up. I wanted to believe this, and the way she enthusiastically jumped into our "relationship" made me believe her.

We were practically inseparable for a couple of months. I have a number of photos of us walking around Manhattan. We have several old-school selfies we took of ourselves in which we look happy—dare I say, in love.

As the sales training program came to a close, it was clear that Gwen was in the top of her class and could choose to work at any of our company's offices—meaning she could work at the NYC office if she so wished. Not everyone had this honor, and I thought for sure she would want to stay. But she wanted to go back to Minnesota.

At first, we talked about me visiting Gwen shortly after she moved back to see how I liked her state. I was getting excited about the prospect of moving there to begin a life with her.

I started planning how I was going to tell my mom that I was in a relationship with a woman and would be moving across the country to live with her. My heart would race just thinking about it; I felt as if I had figured out who I was and where I was going.

Once Gwen was back in Minnesota, the time between our calls started to expand. She broke it to me that she and her girlfriend had decided to try to make things work. Had she and her girlfriend ever really been at risk? Had I stood a chance, or was our relationship essentially a way for her to have fun while in the big city? I didn't ask.

I was a wreck. I stayed in my room sobbing in bed for hours, for days, for weeks. Oscar was my roommate by then, and he was worried about me. Then he grew frustrated that I wasn't getting over myself. So, he dragged me out to a gay bar, and the healing began, as it often did, with a drink. I think I may have even danced on the bar that night.

These days, I can go months or years without thinking about Gwen, and then something will remind me of her. I might check her out on Facebook, and there she is, looking like that successful, got-her-shit-together woman I was wild about.

That a woman as self-possessed as Gwen wanted to be with me had made me feel significant. When she withdrew her affection, I felt lost and undeserving again. Now, I'm grateful. I wasn't ready for a big life-altering move. I was a jumble of insecurities and fantasies at the time, and being a lesbian was a potential identity that might make me feel relevant.

My bad luck with women would continue into the next

decade. Looking back, I think that perhaps women were more capable of seeing how much work I might be!

Work, Part II

When I first got to New York at the age of twenty-one, I had no clue how hard it was going to be to find a job. Turns out I hadn't applied myself very well in college. I had concentrated on partying, so I had a diploma to show for myself and not much else. I hadn't submitted to the college literary magazine, and I had written exactly one article for the school newspaper. My jobs during college were completely unrelated to my dream of becoming a published writer. I also sucked at typing and was highly offended that this mattered to the employment agencies I was visiting.

In the late 1980s, *Sassy* magazine was all the rage with teens and young women, and I was a big fan. Their offices were in Times Square, not far from where I lived, so I decided to apply for a job at the magazine. I don't know why I thought they would want to interview me, let alone hire me.

I went to the stationery store and picked out a sheet of thick lime-green paper for my résumé and a matching full-size envelope. That was where my strategy for working at *Sassy* magazine ended. I had nothing desirable to offer them. Not even a lousy *cum laude* (I had finished college with a 3.421 GPA).

I ended up working at a television representation firm throughout most of my twenties, first as a sales assistant and then in the ratings research department. I did well, but I always felt a step behind where I should be for my age.

While working at the rep firm, I met Natalie, who became a close friend. Natalie was a few years younger than me and had that professional poise and drive that I was certain I lacked. When we worked in research together in the early 1990s, she was promoted to manager before I was, as was my boyfriend at the time.

This boyfriend and I were up for the same promotion. Since the research department supported the sales department, in addition to being interviewed by the research director, we also had to meet with the manager of the corresponding sales team. I arrived at the sales manager's doorway for the interview and waited for him to notice me.

He looked up from his desk and said, "Come in, sweetheart."

I knew right away I wasn't getting the job. I was correct.

A year later, at the age of twenty-seven, I finally locked down a manager's position, working for a formidable woman manager who accelerated the process of toughening me up.

Producing quality work and filling my portfolio with thank-you memos from the sales team provided a much-needed boost to my self-confidence. Work became the arena where I proved to myself that I was smart, capable, and resourceful.

At the same time, as I walked the halls of our office, I never knew when I might bump into a guy I had slept with—the list was growing. I also made a few drunken passes at straight women and otherwise acted foolishly too many times to count.

I wasn't the only one messing around, mind you. The sales reps were having flings with each other, and rumors went around about married sales managers bedding sales assistants.

One assistant, folks whispered, had been transferred to another office in order to move her away from the highly placed man who was done with her. Was that a thing—transferring an assistant to another city? I preferred to imagine that she had left of her own accord.

To my chagrin, I was learning that appearance and clothing were important in the workplace. I've never had a real distinct sense of style, and I'm happy to dress anywhere along the spectrum from "feminine" to "masculine"—so long as I look good *and* feel comfortable.

One of the research directors spoke with me several times about my fashion choices. She didn't like my low-heel wingtip ankle boots, which I often wore with black pants, or my favorite outfit, which consisted of a dark burgundy wool vest and matching dressy shorts, worn with dark tights, a button-down white shirt, and a men's-style necktie with a paisley print in fall shades.

This woman had a collection of short skirts in an array of bright colors and matching pumps that showed off her long legs. She suggested that I should wear dresses and high heels more often.

Being told what to wear did not sit well with me, and I didn't have a lot of money to go out and buy new clothes that weren't me, so I didn't much follow her suggestions. That boss was not the only person during my early work years to emphasize to me that I needed to look more "professional"—which for a woman meant finding that sweet spot that wasn't too casual, frilly, slutty, prudish, bohemian, butch, punk, or sporty. Definitely no Spice Girls allowed in the corporate world.

Every year, this same company held a managers' conference in a resort location. My friend Natalie convinced the CEO that the research managers should be included in this conference, along with the sales and programming managers who had always attended. So, not long after I was promoted to research manager in 1993, our department was invited to give its first-ever presentation at this conference.

I was instrumental in the decision to model our presentation on the half-hour television infomercials that many of our client stations aired late at night. Our team of eight or so research managers worked hard on that presentation, practicing it over and over, and keeping it secret from the other departments as best we could. It was clever, informative, and relevant, and it gave each manager a chance to shine. It had a series of prerecorded clips that we had solicited from various station managers, which popped up at key moments in the presentation, plus a funny clip at the end that we knew would go over well.

The team had agreed that I would play the host of our infomercial. Given my level of introversion and anxiety, I don't know how I managed to secure that part. Probably no one else wanted to do it. I was about twenty-seven or twenty-eight at the time, and I was kind of excited to have the lead role in such an important presentation.

The conference was in a beautiful hotel in Mexico. (All expenses paid! Thanks, Natalie!) About an hour before the presentation, we were doing a run-through in the empty meeting room, which would soon be full of sales managers from around the country, including the top brass from our headquarters.

In case you haven't seen an infomercial, I should note that the host is usually upbeat, persuasive, and a little cheesy—like a motivational speaker. I was going to start the presentation by talking in a conversational tone to the audience while walking casually down the center aisle between their chairs, and then back up to the front again.

I mentioned to the other managers that I was terrified, and a woman offered me a pill to help me relax. I don't know why I didn't ask what it was before taking it. This woman was pretty straitlaced, so I thought it was just a Valium or a muscle relaxer. My family always had a lot of pills in the house, and I had sampled our Valium and Demerol at a young age without any adverse effects.

The presentation was a huge hit. We got lots of kudos from the sales managers and even from the notoriously smug programming managers. It was an incredible feeling.

We were scheduled to do an outing in Cancun within an hour, so we all went back to our hotel rooms to get changed. My new boyfriend (also a research manager) went with me to my room, where I proceeded to lose it. I started crying, and I swear I could not stop. In all my years of bawling my eyes out, I've never cried like that. Every ounce of stress from the presentation and from twenty-eight years of life was flowing out of my eyes. My boyfriend, Greg, was concerned and did not want to leave my side. I told him to go on the tour because I needed to ride this out by myself.

That night our company held a fancy banquet in the hotel. Outside the ballroom, Greg cornered the woman who had given me the pill.

"What the hell did you give Lisa before the presentation?" he nearly yelled.

"It was one of my dad's blood pressure pills," she explained, her eyes wide.

Greg's face was really red. "What were you thinking? She had a really bad reaction to it!"

"Oh my god, I'm so sorry. What happened?" She looked genuinely aghast.

"It's ok," I said, trying to smooth things over. "I'm fine now. I just had a bit of a breakdown in my room."

I never did ask why this woman was carrying around her

dad's medication. But I did learn a number of lessons on that trip: (1) I shouldn't take mystery pills, even from seemingly trustworthy people; (2) I might benefit from finding a more effective way to relieve my anxiety; (3) even though it made me nervous, I did like speaking in front of people; and (4) Greg was a keeper.

Marriage

In the early nineties, Natalie, Greg, and I started out as TV ratings analysts on the same research team before moving on to manage our own teams. The three of us had become friends, and then one day I started looking at Greg differently. It's so weird how your perspective on someone can shift. Was it there all along waiting for the right conditions to bloom, or did it just burst out of the ground overnight?

I was twenty-seven years old and still dating the guy who had beaten me out for that earlier promotion. I was growing tired of his meeting me at movie theaters and bars already stoned, and I had started wondering if it was time to end things.

One summer night, Natalie and I went to watch a company softball game. My boyfriend was not in attendance, but Greg was there. Everyone went to a pub to celebrate our win, and after numerous drinks and some serious flirting, Greg and I decided to slip out together. I was excited to discover that he, too, had been feeling the shift.

Our connection was more than chemistry. We had *potential*. So, I set about extricating myself from my boyfriend. Once I became officially available, my relationship with Greg advanced quickly. He was nice and smart and funny and stable—all the things I was always looking for in a guy. And he loved me!

In early adulthood, it was important to me that my life not resemble my mom's. I did not want to go it alone. I wanted a husband, an accomplice with whom to take on the messy project of living. Unlike my mom, I wasn't attracted to motherhood; I just wanted to be part of a two-person team of adult equals.

During that work trip to Mexico, Greg and I started talking about getting married. We decided to do a planned elopement. I felt bad about not telling Mom, but I knew she couldn't afford to throw us a wedding—and this would relieve her of feeling any shame or charging up her credit cards.

We got married at city hall in Lower Manhattan, with most of my close friends present. Fun fact: Comedian Andy Richter (known primarily as the sidekick to Conan O'Brien) got married there right before us. Second fun fact: When the official performing the ceremony asked if there was any reason we shouldn't get married, Oscar shouted out, "She's a ho!"

In 1994, not long after getting hitched, Greg and I moved to a charming neighborhood in Brooklyn, which I adored. Six months later, when he got a job offer in Washington, DC, I said yes to the move even though I didn't want to leave my friends and our lovely new apartment. I convinced myself that the move would help me do a reset, get a better job, and fix whatever hole was expanding inside me. Instead, things got worse.

At twenty-eight, I was not ready for marriage. I ended up cheating on Greg multiple times. The first time was early on in the marriage. Experiencing acute guilt, I told him about it, and the fact of it sat there between us for months like an unwelcome guest who refused to go.

I liked Greg's family, especially his mom and his sister; I thought about how they might react if they knew how disrespectful I had been toward him. It made me feel like a monster.

The move to Maryland, the cheating, my issues with intimacy, and my insecurity became intertwined, and the partnership was doomed. I became infatuated with a woman at work, and then another one. For a while, I would get wasted and call Robin late at night after Greg had gone to bed to lament my situation. I now know what it's like to engage in conversations with someone who wants to drunkenly vent about the same issues again and again with little self-awareness. At the time, though, I was not cognizant of what a giant pain in the ass I had become.

Greg and I put off talking about our growing detachment and tried to soldier on. When we finally went to couples counseling, it took less than an hour to realize it was over. We sat in that room with the therapist, and it became clear that neither of us had the will to attempt to fix things. We went home that evening and talked and cried and decided to separate. I called the therapist's office the next day and canceled our second appointment.

I have piles of photos from the six years I was with Greg. Photos from all over the city, photos of us moving into our Brooklyn apartment, photos of us opening presents at Christmas, photos of us hanging out with my friends. In many of them, I look happy. Genuinely happy. Greg was a good guy. I hope he's got a good life now.

When Greg helped me move to a one-bedroom apartment in January 2000, I had no idea how much pain and growth were ahead of me. It was just me and my cat Nigel. At the age of thirty-four, I was both exhilarated and profoundly sad.

Persona: Glossy Woman

I n my early twenties, I became friends with Heather, a
woman I met at work in New York City. Heather was tall
and blonde, with a preppy, girl-next-door look. Her family had
money—they paid for her Upper East Side apartment and the
majority of her expenses. Her salary was mostly used for recre-
ation, meaning dinners out, drinks, and drugs.

After work one night, we were at a local restaurant for
happy hour. She and I were waiting for beers at the bar when
she nodded her head toward a woman at the other end.

"Ugh, I wish I looked like her," Heather said.

"Tell me about it!" I replied.

I was stunned because I had assumed Heather's wealth
made her immune to envy.

This woman's light brown hair had the perfect proportion
of chunky blonde highlights for that time period. Her
eyebrows were well-groomed; her makeup was pristine; her
skin was warm and glowing. She had a French manicure and
expensive-looking gold jewelry that included tasteful diamond
stud earrings. Her clothes were a flawless blend of feminine
and professional, and her body was a balance of slim, shapely,

and toned. Her polished look conveyed that she spent the appropriate amount of time and money on her appearance. Also, I could tell she had a raw beauty that made the work easy. This woman may have had her own struggles, but from my barstool she looked blessed.

For the last four years, I had been side-eyeing the glossy women, as I called them. My college enrolled lots of them. I knew that even if I had access to a manual that would clue me in on all their secrets, I could not pull it off. My cheekbones were nonexistent, my nose was blobby, and my hair refused to lie flat. I always had a ragged hem on my skirt, chipped finger-nails, and the wrong shoes. Most of all, I did not want to put in the effort it would take to master such a look.

I still coveted the result. So did Heather. Which surprised me, because if anyone had access to the specifications of the regimen and the funds to take on such a challenge, it was Heather.

I was delighted to know that rich girls could be jealous of other women and that they, too, might think that putting on the feminine uniform wasn't worth the hassle.

In 2014, a contestant on one of my favorite guilty pleasure TV shows, *Survivor*, gave me a glimpse into the mind of a woman for whom the hassle was a rule, not an option. She was a former NFL cheerleader, and on a remote island with few resources, she managed to look gorgeous at all times.

At one of the "tribal councils," where the competitors often confront each other, this woman accused another woman of being jealous of her and stated for the record that she thought any woman could look hot if only she tried hard enough. The ex-cheerleader did not understand why a woman wouldn't want to maximize her appearance to its full potential. It dawned on me that to a woman trained to be competitively attractive, it bordered on negligence not to suit up for the game.

That night in the bar, Heather and I briefly bonded over our conflicted feelings about playing the beauty game to the best of our ability. Then we sighed and went back to our beers.

Persona Add-On: Sex Enthusiast

I don't have to tell you this, but sex is everywhere. At the time when I was waiting for puberty to kick in, I started noticing that almost every song was about sex. My friends and I also had our pick of movies about horny teens figuring out how to get laid (and, if the movie was any good, how to deal with the ramifications of having sex).

Fashion magazines and the beauty industry promised to heighten my sex appeal, while advertisers capitalized on my preoccupation with sex to sell me their products. Attractive young women were often presented as synonymous with sex.

It would be hard to overstate how huge Brooke Shields was when I was a teen. She was born the same year as I was, and she was physically stunning—she could look innocent or mature, often both in the same photo. At the age of fourteen, Brooke was on the cover of *Vogue* magazine and in a commercial for Calvin Klein jeans, saying, "You want to know what comes between me and my Calvins? Nothing."

The message I received was that being sexy was very important for women. If a guy wanted to have sex with you, that was the best form of flattery. And just as I was finally becoming sexually interesting to boys my age, our society was deciding that it was okay for women to want sex ourselves. But we had better be good at it.

In high school, kids would say that a girl was a "dead fish" if she just lay there during sex. I worried for a long time that I was a dead fish. I was very self-conscious about my body and what I was supposed to do. Sometimes I just froze up and waited for it to be over.

I wanted to be sexually free and insatiable, like the female characters who were popping up on TV and in books and movies. I'm not talking about someone who looks sexy (though I wanted that too, of course)—I'm talking about someone who really enjoys sex. You know how a friend reports that they spent the entire weekend in bed with their latest flame? Yeah, that's not me.

My sexuality was and is a swirl of contradiction. I don't like wearing tight, revealing clothes, but I do like to dance provocatively. I am happy to talk openly about sex, yet many of the things I'm typing right now I've not discussed outside a therapist's office.

During my prime hookup years, my standards were pretty loose, so I have a high overall tally of partners. I've been with both men and women, had sex with people who were much younger than I as well as much older, participated in several threesomes plus one sex party, and been up for light role-playing when the time was right.

On a dare from a kooky friend with whom I hung out briefly in NYC, I answered a personal ad in the *Village Voice* newspaper from a couple looking for a woman to join them for some frisky fun. I met them at a bar and even accompanied them to their apartment, where the guy promptly got on the phone and never got off. The woman told me I could leave, and she wished *me* good luck as I walked out the door! (I'm pretty sure I would have bailed on these strangers myself before things progressed.)

I might have had a creative outlook on the subject of sex,

but as for the actual mechanics, the stuff you do with your body parts, I was pretty humdrum.

From the time I lost my virginity at sixteen after my junior prom through to my mid-twenties, sex was primarily about seeking validation that I was desirable. Getting someone to sleep with me was like a sport. If I hadn't drunk so much throughout my single years, I doubt I would have had sex with quite so many people. Alcohol made me bold for the hunt and then calmly disconnected during the reward. Sex was satisfying on occasion. Mostly, it was for bragging rights and a sense of adventure.

It's not as if I'm incapable of having intense, beautiful sexual experiences. Given the number of sexual encounters I've had, though, my return on investment has been slim.

I didn't have trouble achieving orgasm; in fact, that might have been part of the issue. I didn't feel that I needed to get someone in my bed to take care of that need. I could make myself come pretty easily—I'd been doing so since I accidentally figured out how while climbing up a pole on the swing set in my backyard around the age of ten (oh, my poor neighbors).

What I couldn't take care of myself was kissing. I sincerely contend that lengthy kissing sessions with someone new are one of life's great pleasures. At the beginning of a sexual or romantic connection, when it was all about the discovery and the conquest, fooling around was exciting to me. As soon as shit got real, my mind and body short-circuited.

Deep attachment and physical abandon did not mix well for me. During my first marriage, sex became so uncomfortable emotionally that I started crying in the middle. I was convinced that I was a failure. I hadn't figured out the secret to being good in bed, relaxing and having fun, pleasing my partner, and pleasing myself.

My issue with sex was one of the main reasons I started therapy at the age of thirty-two. Counseling and building up my self-esteem have helped. This part of my personal journey is still very much in progress. I am making an effort to get in touch with the side of me that longs for *genuine intimacy*, not validation. I would like to be friskier in bed, more playful, and lustier. Or, I could simply try accepting who I am instead of comparing myself to some idealized persona.

In the meantime, I'm not going to write a sex tips book anytime soon.

Four

DORMANCY

Drinking, Part I

My first experience drinking alcohol was on a summer trip to stay with my friend Amy, who had moved away two years earlier. Amy and I had gotten close during the BOP Club years, when Robin and Julia were otherwise occupied and before Shannon moved to town. Amy's family moved around a lot, so we tried to keep the friendship going by flying to see each other. We were both thirteen years old when I arrived for my second annual visit and discovered that Amy was now half a foot taller than me.

That summer Amy and I spent a lot of time with her new friend Pam, whose family ran a golf course and owned horses, which seemed incredibly glamorous to me. We careened around the course in a cart, taking beer to the golfers. The three of us snuck into a deserted barn and mixed beer with orange juice. We laughed and danced around. I tried to act like I was tipsy. The truth is, I hated the taste and couldn't consume enough to get buzzed.

Amy had a crush on Scott, a nineteen-year-old guy (a man!) who worked at the golf course. Knowing that she liked someone who was so much older stirred up anxiety, longing, and jealousy inside of me. When I met Scott, I was shaking and couldn't meet his eyes. He was cute and very funny. Amy and I giggled at every joke he made. Once I got used to being around him, I looked forward to our visits to the golf course.

I especially liked it when he accidentally brushed against my arm or said my name. Afterward, I would think maybe I shouldn't like it so much.

One of my last memories from the trip was of Scott massaging Amy's shoulders. On the flight home, I thought of Amy spending time with Scott and how I didn't need to be wearing the bra I had on.

A couple of weeks later, a letter arrived from Amy revealing that she and Scott had kissed. I cried over a guy for the first time that day, because I was envious and because I was convinced that I would always look like a little girl and no one would ever want me.

For several years, I watched as my best friends matured and the boys began to circle. By the time boys did start noticing me, when I was about fifteen, I had missed out on that precious time when hormones are starting to flow but sex is not yet on the table. If I wanted to join in the fun, I was going to have to jump into the deep end of the pool without any prep time on the shallow side.

Suddenly I had these curves that had appeared out of nowhere, and I was supposed to be comfortable with boys touching me when I was freaked out seeing my new body in the bathtub.

Alcohol came along right at the time when I felt that I could use some manufactured courage. I don't recall being exposed to other solutions for building up my confidence. If alternate solutions *had* been communicated to me, they hadn't made an impression.

Almost everyone was drinking by age sixteen, so despite

my very conservative upbringing, I didn't question whether to drink or not. I just *did*.

After so many years of being seen as a misfit or a nobody, I believed that I was a somebody when I had a drink in my hand. Without realizing it, the little girl from the family that didn't drink had absorbed the pervasive fairy tale about the magic of alcohol. I had learned that drinking is a marker that you're no longer stuck in the embarrassing confines of childhood. Saying yes to alcohol would rid me of the stink of innocence and immaturity.

Teen movies almost always included a scene or two of boisterous drinking. It's not as if I witnessed a character in a movie chugging alcohol and then went right out and started drinking. Still, there is little doubt that the deluge of images promoting alcohol seeped into my subconscious over time.

Every weekend my friends and I attended parties where the main purpose was to drink and fool around. Getting drunk with my friends was a way to cut loose, bond, and celebrate being alive.

It didn't take long before I made out with a guy I barely knew at a party; I never would have kissed him while sober. This became a frequent practice—let's see who I'll end up with tonight! Often, I felt shame when I woke up the next morning and remembered whom I had hooked up with or learned from my friends some stupid thing I had done. Then I did it all over again the following weekend.

Alcohol produced desirable results—a sense of warmth, self-assurance, and elation—even if those feelings were short-lived and deceiving. In addition to lowering my inhibitions and making the most boring nights adventurous, drinking helped me tap into some difficult emotions that I had been stuffing down.

Yes, I was *that* girl—the one who frequently ended the night blubbering in the back seat of someone's car. Alcohol allowed me to mourn the fact that I didn't know my father, that my mother suffered from depression, that I didn't feel normal. My resentment would pour out through my tears, and being drunk meant I didn't care who witnessed my meltdowns.

Obviously, this was not a constructive way to address these issues, but it served a purpose—and no one had taught me any other way. I don't think my family, my teachers, or any other adults in my life knew that I was struggling to be a cheerful girl, get good grades, and win the admiration of my peers, all while feeling wholly inadequate. Drinking functioned as both the key to unlock my suffering and the balm to soothe my distress.

~

Right from the start, I experienced all the short-term effects of excessive alcohol use. My self-consciousness evaporated, making me flirtatious and undiscriminating. Often, I became impulsive and belligerent. I vomited. I blacked out. I put myself in unsafe situations. I tolerated nasty hangovers. In fact, I blame a hangover for my much lower than anticipated score on the SATs, something that irritates me to this day.

There I was at sixteen, and my extracurricular activities had been whittled down to cheerleading and partying. And though I never cheered drunk (no way!), I was always in a rush to get out of my uniform after the game and start drinking.

The night before a cheerleader "kick-a-thon" for charity, a group of us got bombed. I still have the photos of us laughing and hanging onto each other at someone's patio table. The cheerleading event was at a mall an hour's drive from home. I spent most of the day in a back room doubled over in pain, going in and out of the bathroom, until our coach called my mom to come get me.

In spite of the ongoing consequences, my friends and I mixed drinking with just about everything. We grew up less than two hours from Disney World, and once we were old enough, we made a trip to the theme park without any parents and snuck in alcohol. A friend got sick while waiting in line for the Pirates of the Caribbean ride. I vividly recall the echoing sound of her vomit splattering on the concrete in the cavernous structure and a boy crying out, "Mommy, that girl is throwing up!"

In addition to neighborhood parties, we started going to bars that were known to have lenient ID-checking policies— anything to get out of the house and go wild. Rarely (if ever) did we have a designated driver on these outings. No one wanted to be the dull sober chick. It's a miracle we never caused an accident. Many Saturday mornings I had to run out to the car before my mom got up and clean up the cigarette ashes and empty cans we had left behind.

The sneaking around, the disappointment in myself that I felt, the fear that I might really screw up—these things were all worth it to me. I was chasing an archetype. My goal was to be the girl in the movie—the star, not the sidekick. The self-assured girl. The girl other girls wanted to be around. The girl who always got the guy in the end.

Alcohol was the next best thing to the dream of moving to a different town and starting over at a new school where no one knew my history as a loser. With alcohol, I hoped to relaunch my high school years as someone fun, outgoing, and popular.

When I was a high school senior, I managed to throw one of those legendary movie-style parties. My grandmother was out of town visiting one of my uncles, and my mom was spending the night at a friend's place. She trusted me alone in the house. So, what did I do? Party!

That night, my house was full of people drinking, and I felt accepted at last. Alcohol was helping me play the part I so desperately wanted to play.

Things got out of hand. People were parking on our front

lawn. Someone staggered into a neighbor's yard, and the cops were called. My best friends ran through the house dumping the booze. Someone had to rouse me from the bathroom floor, where not much earlier I had murmured, "Ouch, Shannon, don't step on me" (which became a catchphrase in our group for a while).

In my drunken state, I somehow convinced the police not to call my mom at her friend's house. She would have been furious if she had had to come home late at night. The next day I told her a slightly tamer version of the story because I knew she was going to hear something from the neighbors, plus the front door had been damaged and was going to need to be fixed before my grandmother returned home.

It was so important that night to leave my dorky, invisible girl status behind at any cost. Alcohol allowed me, even encouraged me, to compromise my values. This would not be the last time it would happen, not by a long shot. And the related shame that gnawed at me would also return again and again.

Each night of drinking was a risk in itself. Strung together, they represented a potential deferred. On the day that club photos were taken for our senior yearbook, Robin and I thought it would be funny to crash several of the photos. In the group shot of the drama club, a male friend who signed my book wrote, "What's Lisa doing here?"

This begs the question, why *hadn't* I been in the drama club or on the yearbook staff? Perhaps because they wouldn't contribute to my campaign for coolness, so I didn't have time for them. The goody-two-shoes girl from my childhood had been buried, and I was dancing on her grave, drink in hand.

Drinking, Part II

My college years were filled with serious drinking, at least three times a week every week. It was practically a required subject. Florida raised the drinking age from nineteen to twenty-one while I was in college. For those of us (like me) who were nineteen or twenty when the law changed, the state kindly allowed us to continue drinking legally. We had a bar on campus, and alcohol advertising was everywhere. The fraternities and sororities took turns holding weekly campus-wide parties with low cover charges and all-you-can-drink beer.

No one in the dorms cared if you stumbled home late and threw up in the toilet. No more sneaking out or worrying about your mom catching you. Not much driving was required—everything we needed to get trashed was within a small radius. College was like an Olympic training camp for drinking, preparing me and many others for an adulthood of medal-caliber boozing.

Trying to imagine college without drinking is like conjuring up a different version of myself. During those four years, I sucked down the identity of "drinker" and let it dissolve into my bones until I felt it was an inextricable part of my personality.

In my sophomore year I joined the staff of the campus newspaper, ready to gain some writing experience. Pasted in my college scrapbook is the lone article I wrote for the paper. On my second assignment, I was supposed to cover a night-time event. It was Halloween, so I went out drinking with my friends instead. I quit the paper the next day, feeling a smidge guilty but mostly okay with my priorities. That same scrapbook contains no fewer than fifteen clippings about campus keg parties and local bars.

I empathize with that young woman who chose partying over developing her writing. I wanted to have a blast in college, and I thought there would be plenty of time to buckle down and lead a work-oriented life after graduation. It was such an innocent move, yet it made a lasting impact. For me, it meant I was totally unprepared to build a writing career after college.

Romantic and sexual interactions at college almost always involved alcohol. If drinking was a subject, then hooking up was a sport, and the goal was to be a high achiever at both. Sex was not to be feared (which is a good thing, right?); it was part of what we were there for, given the wide range of potential partners and no supervision. Alcohol greased the wheels *and* muddied the waters.

Drinking gave me the guts to come onto guys (and women) who might have otherwise intimidated me. Often when I went out, my intention was to drink enough so that I would be liberated to go back to the room of whomever I was crushing on at the moment. Now and again, I went home with someone I barely knew. At the age of eighteen, I had progressed from kissing guys I wouldn't have kissed when sober to having sex with guys I wouldn't have had sex with when sober. And I'm sure plenty of guys had sex with me primarily because they were trashed, as evidenced by the fact that we seldom spoke or made eye contact again.

In my first semester of freshman year, I went with a cute guy to his dorm. I was very drunk, and before I knew it, my clothes were off. I wasn't in a complete blackout; my thoughts were like a constantly shifting kaleidoscope—I couldn't grab on to any single perspective for very long. The guy was proceeding with the act while I was trying to slow things down. He was lying on top of me on his bed, and I was squirming backward until my head was up against the wall and there was nowhere else to go. I think I said no or shook my head. I can't be sure. I do know that I wasn't actively complying. I still find it hard to call it rape, but that's what it was.

The weird and pathetic thing is, I went back and had sex with him later in the school year—this time consensually. I guess I was trying to purge or replace what had come before or take control of the powerlessness I felt whenever I saw him on campus. I do know that neither occurrence would have happened if it weren't for alcohol.

Drinking led me to make many poor choices, including fooling around with people who were committed to others, not to mention betraying my own relationships. I was unable to accept my complicity in these actions because I couldn't stop viewing myself as pitiful. When I was intoxicated, my insecurities combined with the alcohol to unleash a ravenous, clawing need. All that mattered in those moments was extracting proof that I was deserving of affection. I did not respect myself, and I treated others with a similar disrespect because I could not fathom my own power.

~

More than all the hookups, my greatest regret is that I didn't try a wider variety of activities in college while I had the chance. One exception was my brief foray into acting. As part of an effort to step outside my comfort zone, I had taken a speech class and liked it. So, in my junior year I decided to pursue a minor in speech and drama. For this minor, I was required to audition for a play my senior year. The professor had chosen a play with a large cast, so pretty much everyone who tried out got a part. I played Cora, the wistful cafe owner who was having a fling with a younger man.

Rehearsing for and performing that play was one of my most memorable experiences in college. Talent-wise, it was clear I did not have a future in acting, but I loved the camaraderie with the cast and crew.

I was terrified yet exhilarated to go on each night. Even the supporting characters, like mine, had a scene or two in the spotlight. My role included yelling "Oh God!" seven times and then collapsing in a heap on a barstool to end the first act. One night, I slammed my hands onto the stool so hard that I heard someone in the audience laugh. My character also had a scene where she expressed her yearning to leave her small town. Cora's sadness and longing were hard to nail, and when one of my performances was particularly moving, my castmates congratulated me backstage.

This story wouldn't be complete without adding that I managed to get drunk at all the after-parties and sleep my way through half the male cast.

Ultimately, I studied just enough to graduate with a vague sense of pride. I could have done better. Was it fun? Sure. Would I do it again? I can't say.

There is little doubt that those first six years of drinking in high school and college formed pathways in my brain that were nearly impossible to ignore and only grew more entrenched as I covered the same ground repeatedly.

I left college with a particularly sticky drinking habit and a self-confidence deficit that I carried into the wider world.

Fear of Death and OCD Tendencies

As much as I blame societal conventions and media messages for making me constantly question myself, my own mind plays its part, too. Human brains in general are wired to be on the lookout for danger, and mine executes this job with gusto. No preoccupation is too big or too small to take up residence in my mind.

I started to see my first therapist in the late 1990s, when I was around thirty-two years old. We weren't getting anywhere because I was eating up all my time processing trivial complaints. So, she decided we should try anti-anxiety medication and sent me to a psychiatrist who could write a prescription.

On the form that went to my health-care provider, this psychiatrist noted that I had obsessive-compulsive disorder (OCD). She had not told me that she made this diagnosis, so I theorized that she put it down so insurance would cover my Zoloft.

I was almost embarrassed to see those words in print because I didn't believe I had a real problem. As with so many other issues of mine, my OCD tendencies did not rise to a clinical level, although they were like an ever-present annoying friend.

Throughout my life, I gravitated toward rituals that either soothed or intensified my anxiety. I went through phases of collecting various items. I obsessively clipped newspaper articles and photos from magazines, spending hours organizing them into binders (all of which I left in my first husband's basement and never retrieved). I recorded tons of TV shows on VHS tapes (also left behind). Not that long ago, I spent far too much time clipping coupons and spreading them out in little piles across the table before putting them into the multiple tabbed envelopes that I brought with me to the grocery store.

Numbers have always held power over me. I count things that do not need to be counted, such as how many crackers are left in the box or how many seconds I pee.

My mother suffers from a similar strain of this condition. She still has an obsession with doing laundry, and her couch is so piled up with magazines and mail that she barely has space to sit down. Whenever I go down to her basement suite and once again find the kitchen faucet running while she's in the bathroom, I get peeved. As if she has any more power over these weird behaviors than I do!

My fear of death was high up on the list of issues that drove me to start seeing my second therapist at the age of thirty-six. As much as I disliked getting caught up in a vortex of dread, I was so familiar with it that it felt right. It belonged to me. It *was* me.

The prospect of dying in my sleep was particularly scary. This started at a young age and still flares up from time to time. I would close my eyes and almost immediately start to panic that I might die during the night. That thought would lead me to wonder what happens when you die. My heart would start beating faster, and I could feel a river of blood thumping inside my ears—often I could feel the vibration from within my ears on the pillowcase. My stomach felt like one of those bingo cages being spun around and around as I pondered the possibility that I might die and never think another thought again. I would be gone, forever. Just like falling asleep—fade to black. I spent many hours lying in bed getting myself all worked up and then having to talk myself down until sleep finally came. There was one crappy summer in particular, after my freshman year of college, when I hardly slept while it was dark—the night and death tightly linked in my mind.

Bizarre scenarios haunted me in daylight as well. Driving, flying, or anything that involved speed plus other people's skill and judgment made me anxious. If I was tweezing a stray eyebrow at a red light and then put the tweezers in the cup holder when the light changed, I might imagine getting in an accident and the tweezers plunging into my eye.

I worried that I might stab myself intentionally with a knife. I wasn't actually thinking of stabbing myself—rather, I worried that I *might* one day consider it. It was like being one degree removed from wanting to harm myself.

When Greg and I first moved to Maryland in 1995, I went through a period where I imagined an intruder hiding in our apartment waiting to attack me. If I arrived home from work before my husband, I would look under all the beds and inside the closets. I'm not sure what I was going to do if I encountered this ax murderer, but I couldn't relax in front of the TV if I didn't do my checking first.

I am happy to report that I now go long stretches without thinking about dying, and when my fear of death does rear its ugly head, I am able to shut it down before it gets very far by practicing deep breathing and grounding—both skills that I've borrowed from meditation.

If I were to see a therapist today, I might qualify as having body-focused repetitive behaviors (BFRBs). I used to play with my hair a lot as a kid and teen—this involved taking a chunk of my long curly hair and twirling it around my finger until it became smooth, and then rubbing that smoothness against my lips. When I hit my mid-twenties, I became convinced that I was losing too much hair. I would pull lightly at the ends and inspect how many strands clung to my fingers. Then, I might grab a handheld mirror and study the crown of my head in the bathroom mirror, looking for bald spots.

In my early thirties, I started saving the strands that came out during a shampoo. I had this vague idea that if my hair ever got really sparse, this stockpile could be made into a wig. I would do this for about six months, realize how ridiculous it was, and stop. Then, a year later or so, I would happen upon a shoebox stowed away under the bed or in a corner of the closet, and it would be full of wadded-up tissues containing clumps of hair. Full of shame, I would throw away the box. After more time elapsed, I would again become convinced that baldness was just around the corner, so I would start saving hair again. I found my last box about five years ago and stopped for good. Other behaviors have been harder to kick.

Possibly my worst BFRB is picking at the thick skin on my feet. I might be sitting at my desk at home, anxious about something I'm writing. With partial awareness, I'll slip off my sock and start picking at any accessible crack in the thick skin that builds up on my heels. Pulling off small pieces of skin doesn't usually hurt, not until I get to the point where it starts coming off in longer strips. And then I know I've gone too far. The next day I have to put multiple bandages on my foot, and it might hurt to put my full weight on that heel. I often do this while lying on the couch watching TV. I tuck the pieces of skin under the couch cushions, and after a couple of months I have to remember to hand-vac under the cushions before anyone else finds this ghastly collection of foot skin.

Much like a drug addiction or eating disorder, I swear I'm done with picking my feet. I let the skin grow back, and for weeks I put lotion on my feet every night. I'm so pleased when I realize that it has been a month or more since I last picked my feet. I'm hopeful that the pattern is broken. Then, I find myself doing it again, and though I know how painful it will be the next day, I keep it up until my heel is raw. And thus, the cycle repeats itself again.

I've been practicing the same mindfulness techniques that help me fall asleep, and I've been going longer and longer between episodes. Just in case, there's always a box of large Band-Aids in the medicine cabinet.

Drinking, Part III

After graduating college, I drank regularly for three decades. The consumption of alcohol became thoroughly incorporated into my life. I thought about my drinking *a lot*, but it was easy to write off my concerns as those of a consummate worrier.

In my early twenties I decided I wanted to do some volunteer work. I saw an ad in the paper for a suicide hotline that was looking for people to take calls. I inquired and found out that they would train us over the course of two weekends before putting us on the phones. To this day, I don't know why I was drawn to this. As someone who was fully aware of her capacity for anxiety and dread, I'm amazed that I showed up for the training.

At the end of the first weekend, they asked the trainees to attend an Alcoholics Anonymous meeting before our second weekend of training. I guess they wanted us to be exposed to the type of people from whom we might be taking calls? Or maybe they wanted us to see the compassion and acceptance in the rooms?

I was excited to attend an AA meeting. I thought I would

discover at the meeting that I was, indeed, an alcoholic, and that would set me on the road to recovery.

The stories I heard that night convinced me I was overreacting. I was nothing like these people! Of course, I was kinda like them, because I stopped on my way home to buy a six-pack of beer to celebrate the fact that I wasn't an alcoholic.

I attended the second weekend of training for the suicide hotline, and then I chickened out and called to tell them I would not be volunteering after all. Honestly, I think that was the best choice for all involved.

The sense of certainty I got from that AA meeting that I was okay didn't last very long. Instead, I found myself in a conflicted reality that lasted until I was fifty.

I loved drinking and I hated it. There was no ambivalence. Like magic, my body would know that a night of drinking was coming in an hour or so, and it would gear up. My heart rate would increase and my whole body would tingle. I couldn't wait to get that glass in front of me, to take that first sip. You know how when you have to pee so bad, and the minute you enter the bathroom it gets way worse, like, you're going to pee your pants if you don't go *right now*? That's how the buildup to drinking felt to me, especially if it had been more than a night or two since my last drink.

As the first drink took hold, my body and mind would relax. The conversation would immediately get more interesting. Soon the desire for the second drink would start building. How much longer? Should I savor this first one or press on toward the next one? Whether it was with friends or a significant other or by myself, drinking would feel like a mission with its own propulsion.

Occasionally I stopped drinking after two glasses of wine, but the struggle was real. If I proceeded to a third drink, it was

highly unlikely that I was going to stop until I was fully satu-
rated, submerged. Blacking out was common.

This routine went on and on. I drank about three times a
week on average for more than thirty years. I was living what I
call the "just add alcohol" life. For me, booze was the all-
purpose mood enhancer. It tied a big bow on special occasions
—a nice dinner out was incomplete without a cocktail to get
things started and several glasses of wine with the meal.
Really, it went with darn near everything. The list was endless:
beer while playing darts, champagne with oysters, a salted
margarita to start off the night, Bloody Marys or mimosas with
brunch, shots because someone bought a round, a frozen drink
to kick off a summer weekend, red wine in front of the fire-
place, white wine at an outdoor firepit.

My friends and I spent untold hours drinking and laughing
and confiding in each other. In dorm rooms. At bars. In
kitchens. At parties. That distinct loosening of both spine and
tongue, the urgent ordering of another round, the wild
pronouncements, the encroaching fog, the second and third
winds that kept us up into the wee hours.

I never shied away from drinking alone, which became a
cherished custom in my forties. Aaron would ask if I was
coming to bed, and I would say, "I'm gonna stay up a little
longer." This was *my* time—time to be alone, time to relax
without any demands or interferences. One more glass of wine
would turn into the rest of the bottle, and then I might raid my
husband's beer supply.

Some nights I would pass out on the couch, wake up a
couple of hours later, and creep into bed. Other times I would
stay up doing weird things. I don't know where I got the idea
to do these things. They harken back to my days as a kid when
I would play in front of the mirror and visualize being a
grown-up.

Wasted, I would go to a room where hopefully I wouldn't
wake up my husband. If I was in a bathroom, I would sit on

the vanity with my feet in the sink, staring at the mirror. If I was in an upstairs room, I might sit on the floor in front of a floor-length mirror. I would grab my cosmetics case and make up my face as if I were going out. Staring at the mirror, looking at my face, trying to find someone admirable, I would talk to myself and make up weird stories. I would imagine feats of glory, like maybe I was in a dance contest with a talented partner and we were about to wow the audience.

As the night wore on, I would become tired and sheepish, and I would put everything away if I had the energy and then stumble into bed and pass out. The next morning, I might wake up half dressed in bed, not remembering how I got there. I would nonchalantly scan the house for my make-up bag and a mostly full wineglass or beer bottle stained with fresh lipstick.

Not every night ended like this, but it happened often enough that the disappointment in myself became etched deep inside.

I started marking in the back of a notebook what nights I drank and how many glasses I consumed. Those little tick marks glared at me from the page. I made up rules to get my drinking under better control, and then I always broke them.

I suffered many a wicked hangover, including those when I was still somewhat inebriated. Going to work feeling sick to my stomach was the norm. I argued to myself that I didn't drink daily, and I rarely drank before five o'clock in the evening. I never lost a job, suffered any health complications, or got arrested because of drinking. No one ever pulled me aside or contemplated an intervention, though some people probably thought I overdid it from time to time. Alcohol wasn't tearing me apart in dramatic fashion. It was working undercover, confining me to a passive, repetitive, and demoralizing life.

When I was in my forties, I had an early morning gynecology appointment. Normally, I tried not to drink heavily the night before doctors' visits, but this time I messed up.

Appointments with my OB-GYN had to be made months in advance, so I dragged my sorry ass to her office. I shouldn't have been driving; luckily, her office was pretty close to where I lived. Since the doctor would be down at the other end of my body, I was optimistic she wouldn't smell any lingering alcohol on my breath. I said as little as possible and tried to breathe out through my nose.

After the appointment, I was supposed to go into work. I knew it was not a good idea to drive, so I moved my car to a shady corner in the parking lot of my doctor's office, climbed into the back seat, and took a long nap to sober up. My coworkers were aware I had a doctor's appointment that morning, so I knew I could tell them it had run long—very long.

After waking up, as I redid my makeup in the mirror in my car, I felt as if I had hit a new low.

Honestly, much worse had happened to me about ten years earlier, when I was married to my first husband, Greg. I had gone out with people from work in DC and gotten quite drunk. On the cab ride home to my Maryland suburb, I could not articulate to the driver how to get to my house. I was going in and out of a blackout, so my memories are patchy.

I leaned forward from the back seat, trying to figure out where we were. I was wearing a short, loose skirt, and the driver reached back and touched me between my legs. I have a faint recollection of him pulling over, getting in the back seat, and trying to assault me. The sound of him undoing his zipper brought me back to the world, at which point I yelled at him to get back in the front seat. He drove me to the closest convenience store and deposited me there.

The guy working at the counter called the cops to come help me get home. I can only imagine what I looked and sounded like to all these people, these men. The police officer managed to get Greg on the phone, who then came to pick me up. I was just starting to sober up enough to feel completely humiliated.

It fascinates me that scary, embarrassing events like this happened to me and I kept drinking.

As I entered my fifties, the disgrace I felt when I drank too much wasn't even the biggest problem. What ate away at me the most was how narrow and predictable my life had become. How the things I thought I wanted to do weren't going to magically happen without considerable effort on my part, and alcohol was draining the time and energy required for that effort.

Acknowledging this reality to myself didn't change things. Drinking had set down sturdy roots and twisted itself around so many facets of my life. Like the ivy in my yard, it was everywhere. The easiest thing would be to simply let it stay there.

People around me started suffering the effects of their own alcohol use. I've heard that alcoholism is a progressive condition, and I watched it slowly devour a dear friend. I don't think that was the case with me. I'm pretty sure I could have gone on indefinitely, drinking two or three times a week. I tried to get my drinking below that level, trust me. I thought about it all the time. Would this be the week that I might be able to drink no more than once? Could I stop after a couple of glasses of wine tonight? What self-imposed regulation would be the silver bullet?

For thirty-five years, my love of drinking had drowned out my passion for writing. Entertaining myself was more important than challenging myself. Self-doubt whispered in my ear that life was so much easier lived from the couch, where I could sip wine and lose myself in other people's lives on television or my phone. I gave my most energetic hours to my employer, and when I got home, I let alcohol and screens have what was left of me.

The joy I got from drinking withered, and I could see my potential fading. The cost of keeping alcohol in my life began to outweigh the benefits it delivered. If this were a work-related dilemma, it would be a no-brainer: time for a new strategy.

Climbing out of such a well-worn rut would not be easy. I wanted to write, really write, and try new things, and get healthy and strong. I wanted to move toward a more promising future, and at long last I suspected it was going to be so worth it.

And then, in April 2017, an acquaintance in recovery shared an essay on Facebook that gave me the final shove I needed. That piece now appears in the book *We Are the Luckiest: The Surprising Magic of a Sober Life* by Laura McKowen as a chapter titled, "The Wrong Damn Question." McKowen writes: "We feel like we need a real reason to not drink, as if a clear mind, a clear heart, and a still, small voice urging us to stay present are not enough."

I was sitting on the couch, and as I read the last line of the essay (which I won't reprint here), I jumped to my feet and shouted, "I'm going upstairs to work on my blog!"

One month later, on May 12, 2017, I stopped drinking for good at the age of fifty-one.

The Train to Hell

A ll my obsessions, fears, and bad habits were like a train ride to hell.

Imagine standing on a train platform. A rickety old train pulls in, and the engineer sticks their head out and hollers, "Train to hell!" The engineer looks maniacal, and the train is clearly unsafe. You've been on this ride before, so you know the tracks are damaged and the route travels alongside the edge of crumbling cliffs.

You say what the heck and get on. After all, you know what to expect, and it gets your adrenaline pumping. Some friends might be on the train, too, so that should be fun.

The ride is as scary as you remember—you are often hanging onto the seat in front of you for dear life. The train makes frequent stops, so you have a lot of chances to get off. You keep going—just one more stop, one more stop.

You stay on the train until dark clouds fill the sky, the wind howls, and the cliffs grow higher.

You finally exit a couple of stops before hell, the sound of the engineer cackling loudly as you collapse on the platform. As you wait for another train to take you back to where you started, you swear you're never going to get on this train again.

Sound familiar? To me it brings to mind a night of heavy drinking, getting in an argument with a friend or lover, or panicking about dying in my sleep. I know I shouldn't go there, yet I do. I live to regret it. I promise myself that it won't happen again. And then it does.

It takes time and repetition to break out of this pattern. I must choose not to participate in the routine over and over. It gets easier. Eventually I notice that I haven't seen the train in a long time. This doesn't mean it might not make an appearance. But I've taught myself to let it leave the station without me on it.

Note: Though I was not consciously inspired by Laura McKowen to write this brief chapter, I wish to acknowledge that she has a chapter titled "Stop Getting on the Train" in her book We Are the Luckiest. *I wrote my extended train metaphor nearly a year after reading her book, and our respective chapters are quite different, but in the event that I was subliminally influenced, I tip my hat once again to McKowen.*

Two Years of Misery

The two years spanning from January 2000 to January 2002 were tumultuous, to say the least. Greg and I separated at the beginning of 2000.

At the age of thirty-four, I was living alone voluntarily (mostly). I had a nice-sized one-bedroom apartment, and I loved being by myself much of the time. But I was a wreck. I knew it was mainly my fault that the marriage had ended, and I was sure that I was too old to find another decent person to love me.

I started experiencing what I think was acid reflux—I was too scared to go to a doctor to check it out. I did not have a car, so I used to walk between my apartment and the metro station to commute to and from work. On the walk, I would start gagging and have to lean over and throw up a little bit on the side of the road or in the parking lot of the train station. I was on a kick of eating Toaster Strudels with scrambled eggs in them for breakfast, and I would often vomit up a portion of that meal. Brushing my teeth and smoking cigarettes also brought on the nausea. I would stand outside with my coworkers on a smoke break and hope they didn't see me trying to stifle my retching.

As time marched on and I became more acclimated to my situation, the reflux stopped. Still, I was unhappy. I had thought when my husband and I got separated that I might start a relationship with a woman I knew from work. I had developed serious feelings for her, and it seemed as if she felt the same way. The few times we tried to take it beyond kissing, it didn't feel right. Then, she decided to fully commit to a relationship with a man she had known for years, and the door was officially closed for me.

I was drinking a lot. I would buy a bottle of wine on the way home from work and drink it all in my apartment while listening to Fiona Apple or watching TV. Once the bottle was empty, I craved one or two more drinks before bed, so I would walk from my apartment into the parking lot of the shopping center next to my complex. Once on the other side of the parking lot, I would weave through a couple of trees, cross a small road, and enter the beer and wine store. I would purchase another bottle of wine or a six-pack of Rolling Rock, convinced that the guy who worked there recognized me and was judging my drinking.

In that shopping center next to my apartment complex, there was a huge bar that had like twenty pool tables and a bunch of dartboards. I would go there by myself and chat up guys at the bar. A couple of times I brought guys home and somehow managed to merely talk with them. I often forgot to pay my bill and would have to retrieve my credit card and close my tab the next day. The head bartender there was running out of patience with me—I could see it in the way he sighed and made as little eye contact as possible.

I was spending more money than I was making. I couldn't afford the rent at my apartment, not with all the alcohol and cigarettes I was buying. I had started putting food at the convenience store on my credit card, digging myself into a hole.

I dated two guys during those two years—Frank and Chase

—and they couldn't have been more different. Frank was a little older, successful, and looked great on paper. We got along pretty well, though there was no real spark. Plus, he was dating at least two other women, and one night he called me by the wrong name on the phone, so that was that.

Then there was Chase, who was much younger than me and had tons of issues. Sex with him was exciting and sorta sleazy. Our whole thing was sketchy. He wasn't physically abusive, but he was controlling and emotionally abusive, and I knew it needed to end. I had started cutting myself around that time—nothing big, dragging a chef's knife along my thigh only enough to break the skin and leave a temporary mark. Luckily, I snapped out of that behavior pretty quickly when I saw the look of disgust on Kelly's face when I showed it to her.

I had sent Chase packing before September 11 happened, and my dear cat Nigel had died that year, so I was alone in my apartment and scared. In the days after 9/11, I started sleeping on the couch with the TV on all night. I had also gone back on Zoloft recently, and the first couple of weeks on the medication got me amped up. This was not a good combo, along with the paranoia that another attack was imminent. I was working in Washington, DC, in an office building about a block and a half from the White House, and many days I had to force myself to go into work.

The two-year period ended with a bang. I should have expected nothing less. Remember that New Year's Eve debacle I teased you with earlier? The time has come to explain what happened that night.

My friends and I met at Kelly's home in Connecticut around noon on December 31, 2001, and just about everything that could go wrong did. (Fortunately for Julia, she couldn't be there.)

The septic system in Kelly's house was backed up by early evening, and we had to pack up all our food and booze and go rent a couple of hotel rooms; otherwise, no one would have been able to go to the bathroom.

Shannon was so out of it that we were sure she was on some kind of drug. As we got drunker, we decided to confront Shannon about her condition, and it turned into a screaming match, most of which I barely remember because I was so drunk. I do recall experiencing that horrifying feeling that made me want to break things and bang my head against the wall.

The next morning, I felt a hollowness in the pit of my stomach. My soul ached. I was certain I had lost my closest friends for good.

On the Amtrak ride home, the train was crowded with people returning to the DC area from the Northeast. I walked up and down the full length of the train a couple of times looking for an empty seat. I got up the nerve to ask a woman who had an empty seat with a book on it next to her, and she let me sit down. We started talking about ten minutes into the ride and never stopped. She was a primary care physician, and she knew all the right questions to ask me to pull out my pain, fear, and sadness. I told her I was considering moving back to New York to help Shannon, and she told me it sounded like I should focus on taking care of myself. She gave me her therapist's name and convinced me to get back into therapy.

As I've acknowledged, I'm not a very spiritual person, yet I think of that woman as an angel who was sent to me at the right time, when I needed her most. She convinced me to concentrate on my own needs. She helped me to see how I kept putting myself in unhealthy situations. She made me feel hopeful that I didn't have to go on like this. (Oh, and she looked a little like my favorite author, Lorrie Moore.) I called that therapist the next business day, and I had my first appointment within a week.

January 1, 2002, broke the spell of those two years and

placed me on my current path. At thirty-six, I still had so much growing up to do, but I was starting to see the way.

Losing a Friend

My friend Shannon, my fellow late bloomer, died of a drug overdose at the age of fifty-four in February of 2020. When she passed, many people from our high school reached out to share personal memories of Shannon. I had a lengthy text exchange with a woman who was on our cheerleading squad. Suddenly I was transported back to a time when cheering and post–football game parties were the highlight of our week.

This woman was one of Shannon's earliest friends in Florida, and she told me: "You guys were cool, and I stayed boring but happy."

Oof. That one hurt. I replied: "Yeah, cool isn't all it's cracked up to be. And for what it's worth, I never felt cool."

For the last couple of years of high school, Shannon and I were both in love with unavailable dudes. Once word got around that she had died, I heard from Shannon's guy. In a text, he wrote: "Shannon was so special. She was one of a kind, a once-in-a-lifetime spirit. I always loved her. She may not have known it, but I did." I hope she knew.

About sixteen years before her death, when we were thirty-eight years old, I started to realize that Shannon's drinking had escalated to the point where every activity, no matter the time, was accompanied by an alcoholic beverage.

In 2004, Shannon and her boyfriend Will helped Aaron and me move into a new apartment. This was something we did for each other many times over the years.

The morning after the move, I noticed Shannon pouring herself a glass of wine in the kitchen. Her hand was trembling a bit. When we arrived at a nearby restaurant for brunch, her eyelids were already drooping and she had lost interest in eating.

About a month later, I was talking on the phone with our mutual friend Oscar, and he agreed that something was up. Each time I talked with a friend about Shannon's drinking, I felt guilty. I needed to give voice to my concerns, but at times it seemed less like processing my feelings or reviewing the options for trying to help her and more like gossiping.

I went to New York in 2005 for a work-related trip on a Friday afternoon, and I planned to stay with Shannon and Will for the weekend. I had agreed to meet Shannon at her office around five o'clock in the evening, and then we would head out to happy hour. When I saw her, I was taken aback. Her face was bloated and red, her eyelids puffy. She was wearing baggy clothes, and her hair was pulled up haphazardly. A large to-go drink container sat on her desk with a seltzer bottle next to it. When we hugged, I smelled alcohol.

As we walked the city streets to get to Shannon and Will's favorite pub, she was swaying slightly. I sensed that she was already buzzed but didn't ask about her state. Shannon offered that she had met Will for lunch that day and had had a couple of glasses of wine. What I smelled emanating from her suggested more recent consumption than lunchtime.

We got to the bar and ordered drinks. I could see that she was not feeling well. Midway through our first or second drink, Shannon got a startled look on her face as if she were about to throw up. She literally looked as though she had been poisoned. Her hand flew up to her mouth, she excused herself, and she shot off to the bathroom.

That whole weekend I felt dread. I remember wanting to be physically close to her, as if that would help. I recall the two of us sitting on the couch drinking and talking. My legs were bent with my feet up on the couch, and I gently slid my toes under her thigh and left them there for a few minutes. It was a weird thing to do, I'll give you that, but it made me feel connected to her, like I could somehow hold her up.

When I went home, I told Aaron how worried I was. A week or so later Shannon and I talked on the phone. She told me how a friend had dropped by her office. At the time, Shannon had been moving heavy boxes around or something and was all flushed (according to her), and the woman asked her if she was taking care of herself. Shannon said to me, "Well, I guess that's another friend I'm not talking to anymore." I took that as a warning not to bring up what I had observed on my visit.

What followed were several years of Shannon being hospitalized and let go from jobs. By 2008, the year Aaron and I planned to get married, things had gotten bad. I was away at a work conference when her boyfriend Will called and told me that Shannon was not doing well—she was out of work and spending all day lying on the couch, drinking, and watching TV. We agreed that Will should call a family member of hers who was in recovery and encourage the two of them to talk. Shannon sure was pissed about that. She did get on the phone that day, though, and agreed to stop drinking.

A couple of months later, Aaron and I were going to help Shannon and Will move apartments in Manhattan. As we were getting ready to drive up there for the weekend, Shannon called and told me that even though she had not been drinking, she was still bloated and looked six months pregnant. I knew she wasn't joking around—Shannon would never issue such a warning unless she was genuinely uneasy about how she looked.

When we arrived, I was alarmed. From the chest up, Shannon looked anorexic. Her eyes were big and sunken in, her hair thin, and her arms spindly. From her upper abdomen down, she looked very pregnant. She was wearing overalls, and her feet were so swollen that she couldn't tie her shoes. She stood up and sat down with great effort, and she was icing down her legs to relieve the pain. Two or three packed boxes sat in the middle of the living room, and that was it. We had only two days to get Shannon and Will moved, so Aaron and I dove right into helping them pack as quickly as possible. I was shaking and felt nauseous. I had a tough time looking at Shannon.

We were forty-two at the time, and I wondered, *How could she have let this happen to herself? Aren't we getting too old to value drinking over our health?* I wasn't drinking enough to end up in a similar condition, so I thought it was okay to expect my friend to get her act together pronto, while I dithered about making and breaking my own rules of moderation.

Shannon told me she hadn't addressed her situation because she wanted to get through this move first. Twice we were visited by people associated with the building that she and Will were vacating. Both times, someone asked Shannon when she was due, and she deftly redirected the conversation.

Over the course of forty-eight hours, I repeatedly made Shannon promise that she would go to the doctor first thing on Monday. This was one occasion when my tendency to fear the worst was no overreaction.

The guys drank many beers over the weekend. I was repulsed by the thought of drinking and couldn't understand how they could do so around Shannon. Truthfully, I couldn't wait to get out of there.

Shannon did go to the doctor soon after we left, and she spent close to two weeks in the hospital while they drained the fluid that had built up in her body. She didn't tell me exactly what had caused her condition, other than to talk about her new super-low-sodium diet. I believe she had ascites, which is typically related to liver disease, but I never pressured her to disclose anything about her health.

When Shannon and Will came to our small wedding a couple of months later, she was completely thin, and part of me was a tad jealous. Not that I wanted to get skinny that way. When my mother-in-law mentioned how "chic" Shannon looked in an outfit she was wearing the day before the wedding, I wanted to scream out, *Do you have any idea what she looked like a few months ago? Are you aware that she's malnourished and likely an alcoholic?!*

The cycle repeated. Shannon would stop drinking, and in a surprisingly short time she would look great and snag a new job. Then she would start drinking again, and it would all go downhill. The jobs started to sound less desirable, and the time she spent at them grew shorter. I can't say for sure how many times she was hospitalized during those sixteen years. Maybe six times? I know Oscar took her to a detox facility once, where she spent about forty-eight hours and then refused to stay for rehab.

Shannon rarely admitted what was going on. She would vent about her issues with Will, or she would complain about the assholes at work. She couldn't bring herself to discuss her own part in how her life was deteriorating. I can recall exactly two conversations when she let down her guard and confessed that she didn't know what to do. She said she didn't feel better when she wasn't drinking. I knew her well enough to know there was no way she would go to AA. I suggested individual therapy, but she was reluctant to see a therapist, saying she was afraid of what might get unearthed.

Shannon and I had more in common from our childhoods than being late bloomers. I had experienced the pressure that comes with being your mother's reason for living, and

Shannon had been the young golden child who carried the burden of uniting a blended family. I wish we would have talked more about the weight of those expectations. From what I could tell, Shannon had learned early on that she needed to project strength and self-reliance; emotions were self-indulgent, and counseling was gratuitous. She had built up a solid facade that rarely came down.

About five years before her death, we were fighting by text, and she called me in the midst of hot, angry tears. It was as if we had struck gold somehow. But we kept going around in circles on the call because she did not want to stop drinking and she did not want to get help.

I started to realize that Shannon and my mom had something in common: They both peered into the abyss, spending time in a world of darkness that I will never know (hopefully). Despite my empathy for Shannon's predicament, I was losing patience. She wanted me to play along that everyone else was at fault for her troubles, and I did my best to oblige her, although I hated pretending. I felt more comfortable expressing my concerns on paper. I sent maybe three letters to Shannon over the course of those sixteen years, attempting to tell her how much I missed our close friendship and how worried I was about her. In an angry phone call one time, she snapped, "Why don't you send me another letter?" So much for that tactic.

Aaron and I bought a house on a lake in 2012, and unfortunately that was the beginning of the end of any shred of normalcy in my friendship with Shannon. When Aaron and I first looked at the place, I immediately envisioned us hanging out there with Shannon and Will. I phoned, emailed, and texted Shannon to plan a visit, but none of the dates I suggested worked, and a few times she didn't respond to my overtures at all. I finally gave up inviting her.

When I first started my blog in 2016, Shannon texted me and said: "Just my opinion, abandon the blog thing. It smacks of narcissism and self-absorption. You're better." I felt as though she had punched me in the gut. I was shaking as I typed out message after message, erasing each one. I settled on "Thanks for your opinion. It's just something I need to do."

No matter what we said or did, Shannon and I never stopped loving each other. When we were in our early twenties, I had a relationship with a mutual friend (nobody mentioned in this book) who should have been off-limits, and Shannon found it difficult to forgive me. Twenty-five years later she brought it up, and I was shocked to learn that it still bothered her. She wanted to know if I regretted my actions. I'm actually glad she finally confronted me and we had the chance to talk about it.

Several years later, Shannon developed an infection in one of her ankles that required multiple operations. Based on my last in-person encounter with her in 2017 and a passing joke she had made about taking "dolls" (pills), I suspect she was prescribed painkillers during this period, which may have contributed to her downfall.

In 2017 Shannon broke up with Will, ending her longest-ever relationship. Her descent quickened. The next year she and I reached a breaking point. We rarely spoke on the phone anymore, mostly communicating by text. Conversations with her had become frustrating and extremely unpleasant; she had a mean streak that could get ugly. I found it more and more difficult not to tell her off.

I was so mad at her for not being able to face what she was doing to herself. She had acquired a long-distance, much younger, bad-boy beau, and she was reveling in the scandal of it all. Her attempts to be clever and cute in our friends' group chat no longer struck me as funny.

Our friend Oscar spent what sounded like a horrendous year living with her. The young boyfriend came for a long visit, and Oscar reported that the situation was dire. I called Shannon's family and tried to get them to intervene, but what could they do? How do you drag a fifty-something woman away from her home and a man?

Shannon was evicted from her apartment in the summer of 2018, losing many of her possessions in the process. She immediately left the country to live with her boyfriend.

The following year, Shannon moved back to Michigan, where her family lived. And that's where she died in 2020. I hadn't talked or texted with her in a while. I did send her a "happy birthday" message in the month before she died, and she replied, "Thanks, Dollface!" (Sometime in our thirties we had taken to calling each other Babycakes and Dollface.)

The phone call came from her ex-boyfriend Will on a Sunday night. He had just heard from someone in her family that Shannon had passed away that morning. I wish I could say I was surprised, but I wasn't. I did feel as if a part of my soul had been ripped from me.

That night I called our friend Robin. Her howls nearly broke me apart. After I assured her it was real and that we would talk later, Robin called Kelly, and I called Julia and Oscar. I spent the next three days in an almost constant state of texting with or calling my friends, various members of Shannon's family, Will, and other people who needed to know before the Facebook announcement was posted.

For weeks, months even, I would recall specific memories and start crying, often while driving alone. One morning, the song "Crying" by Roy Orbison (the version with k.d. lang) came on while I was in the kitchen, and halfway through I fell to the floor sobbing. The song is about the demise of a romantic relationship, but it served as the perfect catharsis for my grief that morning.

As my weepiness abated, I found it hard to get past my anger. I was mad at Shannon. I was mad at her boyfriend, who had been visiting her when she overdosed. I was mad at her family for not finding some magic way to save her. I was mad at myself and mad at our mutual friends. How could she have had so many people in her life who loved her, and still there was nothing we could do?

Shannon had a pattern of fading away and then popping back into our lives without any mention of the time spent out of touch. I suppose it's nice that she felt she could do that—she trusted her friends to forgive her and welcome her back without having to rehash or analyze anything. Even so, I felt she had deserted me, and I felt guilty for *my* part in deserting *her.*

Though our drinking was far apart on the spectrum, Shannon's condition helped me see that I did not want alcohol in my life anymore. I didn't want anything in my life that distracted me from my feelings or pursuing my dreams.

If only Shannon had been more comfortable with self-reflection. This type of "navel-gazing"—examining your actions and the thoughts and stories behind those actions—was not her thing.

Writing *My Unfurling* has been a cleansing experience for me. I only wish Shannon could have found something that would have worked for her in a similar way.

Right up to the end, Shannon insisted she would "figure it out, like always." I do think, to a certain degree, she was okay with the turmoil and the risk if it meant she could live the way she wanted to live. Who knows? Maybe Shannon never would have been content living a sober life of introspection. And I don't know that I could have found a way to fully accept her as she was.

I'm sure we both would have liked a little more time to see if things could have turned out differently, though.

Perhaps we were far more different than I ever imagined. I don't think I knew Shannon the way I thought I did. But I knew the version she wanted me to know, and that was her, too, right? I miss the Shannon who was my friend, and I wish I could have gotten to know the woman behind the mask.

Persona: The Creative Genius

W hen I was around twelve years old, I tested well on an IQ test administered at school and was invited to take a special class for gifted students. I knew I was smart but didn't feel exceptional enough to transcend my humble beginnings.

In the 1970s, my family watched *Donny & Marie*, a popular variety TV show. Toward the end of the show's four-year run, the musical brother–sister duo brought on their youngest sibling, Jimmy.

I was only two years younger than Jimmy, who was about fifteen years old. When he was on-screen one night, I commented to my family that I didn't think he was very talented, adding that I didn't get what the big deal was about him. In my mind, he was on TV because his older siblings were famous.

My mom said in a teasing voice, "Sounds like someone's been bitten by the green-eyed monster."

I hated that expression, and I despised being associated with it. I thought it was obvious that Jimmy Osmond couldn't sing or act. I told my mom she didn't know what she was talking about—I wasn't jealous at all. She and my grandmother gave me the old side-eye and shook their heads.

Of course, I *did* envy people who got a head start in life by being born into rich and famous families. I was also jealous of people with self-motivation flowing out of their pores—people who came from modest families and rose to the top through hard work, grit, and drive.

The media I love to devour—TV, books, movies, music, magazines, and now social media and podcasts—are bursting with creative, compelling people who have figured out how to get ahead in the world and are worshipped for this capacity. Today, thanks to platforms like YouTube and TikTok, the door to fame seems to be wide open.

In the opening credits to the 1980s TV show *Fame*, Debbie Allen tells her students, "You got big dreams. You want fame. Well, fame costs. And right here is where you start paying. In sweat." Yikes!

A part of me has always wanted to skip past the toil and determination part and go straight to being exalted for my cleverness and charm. Without any money or connections behind me, I would have to rely on my own wits and self-discipline, and I wasn't sure I possessed sufficient reserves of either.

Still, the idea of achieving brilliance tantalized me. As a creative writing major, I was encouraged by positive feedback from my professors, but I didn't even attempt to get published in the school literary magazine. I don't recall my adviser or any of my writing professors strongly encouraging me to get my name in print. Maybe someone did and I wasn't listening. I don't know if they could have gotten through to me anyway, as I was more concerned with partying than writing.

A flurry of talented young writers became famous during my college years. The novel *Less Than Zero* was published in 1985 when author Bret Easton Ellis was just twenty-one years old. Jay McInerney (*Bright Lights, Big City*) and Tama Janowitz

(*Slaves of New York*) were also published before they turned thirty. All three of these books were made into big movies. Getting published and making a name for yourself while in your twenties had become a reasonable goal for writing majors.

When I graduated college, someone gifted me the 1987 *Writer's Market* book, which promised to offer thousands of places to sell your writing. Holding this thick book in my hands made me feel like a real writer. Did I ever submit anything to a publication listed in its pages? Nope.

So, what was it that drew me to this persona if I didn't want to ply my craft? I wanted to be the literary chick with the glasses and the tousled hair and the flowy skirts and the pen behind her ear. I wanted to see my name and photo on a book jacket; travel around the country doing readings at cozy independent bookstores; win awards and teach at respected universities; get interviewed on *Today* or NPR; sit around a table with a coterie of deep thinkers, eating and drinking and debating. The idea of a movie version of my book starring Sarah Jessica Parker and Robert Downey Jr. sounded pretty good, too.

As I sifted through my old papers for this book, I saw that I did keep writing after college, though I didn't work to get anything published. I spent considerable time editing a short story called "Wednesdays," printing out multiple versions. At one point I went back and started marking up the novel I had begun in college. Other pages contained stabs at poetry, screenplay ideas, and character studies.

In the journal that I kept briefly in my early twenties, I went off on a fantasy about writing, directing, and starring in a movie about the lives of a group of young women much like me and my friends. In my daydream, I imagined that the movie would be "brilliant." I wrote:

The critics love it, declaring it the most *real* movie about contemporary ordinary lives. ... These are the most complex, fully drawn characters ever. ... Every moment rings true. The performances are heartbreaking, the writing sharp, witty, honest ... very literate. ... By the way, will the movie be nominated, or will it be overlooked, much to the consternation of many a film critic?

Having acted in college, I knew I wasn't a skilled thespian, and yet the fantasy goes on to envision me playing myself. A made-up review heralds me as "natural, gritty, an actress who for the first time expresses many of our secrets."

It's hard not to laugh, right? In the journal I admit that this extended head trip is "vain and horrible but fun," so I think it's safe to conclude that my fantasy was a bit tongue in cheek.

Writing *did* mean something to me. The call wasn't strong enough, though, to win out over my favored distractions.

So, in the long run, I had to drink, watch TV, scroll, and repeat the same old complaints until I was so dreadfully bored that I simply *had* to make space for a writing practice. (Note to self: practice before career.)

In the time since I first held that 1987 *Writer's Market* book, the internet and blogs were invented, so now I could publish my work online. I was in my fifties and flat out of excuses. Early fame and brilliance may have eluded me, but I still had plenty of time to create something satisfying and meaningful.

Five

SECOND BLOOM

Writing and Therapy

Before we jump into the details of how I got unstuck, I want to quickly spell out why disengaging from self-doubt is so critical. I've settled on three broad truisms that are evident throughout *My Unfurling*:

1. Self-doubt impacts your everyday decisions. It can lead to counterproductive habits and unhealthy coping techniques. It can gobble up minutes, hours, and days.
2. Self-doubt impacts your big decisions. It can cause you to forgo your dreams and passions. It can consume months, years, and decades.
3. Self-doubt impacts how you treat other people. As the saying goes, "Hurt people hurt people." And hurt people often see themselves as powerless, making it difficult for them to comprehend their own influence. In this way, self-doubt can devour trust and respect.

I don't think *anyone* is immune to the negative effects of

self-doubt. For many of us, self-doubt is a lifelong struggle. We have to figure out how to manage it, to prune it back. We must not ignore it, but neither should we let it seize control.

Writing has long been a way for me to process uncomfortable thoughts and complicated feelings. For the first half of my life, I didn't fully appreciate that I was doing this—using the act of writing as a form of therapy. So, without the awareness, I wasn't getting the maximum effect from my writing.

After college (and prior to launching my blog), the most consistent form of writing I engaged in was making frivolous lists, sketching out ideas for books or TV shows, starting and abandoning journals, and penning plaintive notes to myself.

My writing was full of questions, including:

- What do I have to do to be noticed and counted?
- Why do I get so angry and frustrated?
- Why do I like drinking so much?
- Why do I want loved ones to feel sorry for me?

I found a piece of notebook paper from about twenty years ago. The page was divided into two triangles by a diagonal line. In the top triangle, I wrote: fun, joy, exhilaration, excitement, possibility, beauty, happiness. In the bottom triangle, I wrote: sadness, loneliness, frustration, hopelessness, anger.

Rather than seeing these feelings as part of the normal range of human emotions, I viewed them as competing for my undying affinity. I thought I had to pick a side: I was either a cheerful person or a miserable person.

I put off reading one particular journal for as long as I could; just looking at the busy black and white design on the cover produced a sinking feeling in my stomach. When I finally mustered the nerve to open it, I was immediately trans-ported back to a stressed-out time in 1989 when I was twenty-four and in between jobs in New York City.

I recall sitting in our kitchen window on West Forty-Third Street writing those entries that veer between mundane, overly detailed accounts of my daily activities and vivid indulgences of hypochondria that verge on paranoia.

I was worried about having leukemia, a heart attack, an aneurysm, a chemical imbalance, diabetes, or an inner ear dysfunction. I was terrified of dying or of losing my memory altogether. I recorded a lengthy list of physical symptoms, including tiny red spots on my skin and my "wandering, frightened mind."

I reported back to my journal that I had visited a doctor, who inspected my spots and decided they were nothing. He suggested that my memory problem was due to stress.

Reading those pages now, it becomes clear that I was caught in a loop of self-perpetuated anxiety, and my drinking wasn't helping. I wrote, "Is it right for a person to keep their mind occupied every minute in order to avoid unpleasant thoughts? Isn't that treating the symptom?"

I feel for that girl. She was often naive, self-involved, tire-some, and juvenile. She subscribed to fatalistic stories about her inadequacy.

A few of my long-running tales included:

- I have terrible luck.
- Life is so unfair.
- There's nothing special about me.
- I'm not ambitious or driven enough.
- My writing is shallow and unsophisticated.
- There's something wrong with me that people can sense, and it drives them away.
- I'm a selfish, self-centered person.

Through writing *My Unfurling*, I sniffed out how those stories materialized and why I grew so attached to them. As important as this work is, at some point I have to stop obsessing over these assumptions and feeling sorry for myself.

Now, instead of spending an inordinate amount of time explaining to myself why the preceding thoughts are wrong, I simply make note that they are past their prime.

- That's an outdated story.
- I'm not going down that road anymore.
- That's an old line of thinking.
- I'm moving past this way of reacting.

I try not to be judgy toward myself, just firm and brief. I forgive myself and utilize the hard-earned self-knowledge I've accrued to move on.

The best part of rehabilitating my brain is that I can be driving along or making dinner and I'll realize that it's been days or weeks since I've gotten lost in one of those "woe is me" black holes. This self-coaching is one of the best gifts I have given myself. Second only, perhaps, to the gift of professional therapy.

My first therapist provided a safe environment where I could start saying aloud the things I had only thought or written about. She made me feel seen and heard. My second therapist meant business—she was not impressed with my superficial gripes and urged me to uncover the primary emotions lurking below. I saw her for three full years in my late thirties, first in private sessions and then in group.

Amidst my old papers, I found a sheet I had typed up for this therapist in December of 2004. It contained a well-crafted proposal stating that I was ready to graduate from therapy. Under six subheads, I crammed a total of forty-one bullets onto a single page.

First, the document reviews the issues that led me to therapy. They included (in my original words):

- anger, frustration, resentment, jealousy (trouble with friends)
- feeling invisible, as though I don't count, and being self-critical
- self-destructive behaviors, including excessive drinking
- OCD-like behaviors, ruminating
- childhood experiences and my desire for answers/feeling owed something for my troubles

As you can see, many of the issues I was resolving back then are still on my radar. Reviewing this sheet sixteen years later, I smile at the insights and connections I was making, such as "asking for what I want instead of stewing" and "giving myself the emotional support I crave (and didn't really get as a child)."

The forty-one bullets on that page are a pretty thorough summary of my troubled psyche and my path toward self-awareness and peace. In the proposal, I promised to "put what I've learned into lifelong practice"—so I had already accepted that the work of building self-confidence would never end. *My Unfurling* is sort of like an updated, expanded version of that page.

I remember handing in the sheet, presenting my case to the group, and hearing my therapist agree that I was ready to fly the nest.

Six years later, I had a few sessions with the same therapist before my mom moved in with me and Aaron, and ten years after that, I would seek counseling online when my friend Shannon passed away.

Therapy (with the right practitioner for you, of course) is all about what you put into it. You have to be willing to *go there*. Whenever I did, I found what I needed.

Work, Part III

At the age of twenty-nine, I started volunteering at NOW, helping with the myriad tasks involved in holding a big demonstration on the National Mall in Washington, DC. I helped put up snow fencing (hard work!), folded endless piles of T-shirts, handed out flyers on busy city streets, and did much more.

Since my catering days, I've been the kind of worker who doesn't mind rolling up her sleeves and doing whatever needs to be done. The nonprofit world loves people with a can-do attitude. My eagerness to jump in and learn new things resulted in an upward career trajectory at NOW. After volunteering for about six months, I accepted an assistant position in order to get my foot in the door. I soon moved up to become NOW's publications manager and then its communications director, a position I held for thirteen years. I worked at NOW throughout my entire thirties and most of my forties!

During my time there, I might be sweating in the basement while stacking up heavy boxes of signs one day and attending a meeting at the Federal Communications Commission the next.

Working at NOW, I learned how to lay out a newspaper in

Adobe PageMaker (the precursor to InDesign), edit images in Photoshop, work with print houses to produce publications, and do basic HTML coding. I took thousands of photos at events on Capitol Hill, in front of the White House, and at countless other locations.

I wrote a lot—press releases, letters to the editor, op-eds, online content, email alerts, newsletter articles, marketing materials, ad copy—and I had to write fast, often while channeling someone else's voice. I produced videos and slide presentations and played a key role at national conferences.

Working at NOW really toughened me up. The national officers I reported to throughout my eighteen years were often perfectionists; several of them had been practicing attorneys and one was a retired Air Force lieutenant colonel. Their standards were extremely high (one might say they lost perspective from time to time regarding the relative importance of various projects), and we were always rushing against the clock. There was no way to stay on track with your to-do list because things were constantly happening in Congress, the media, and the world that needed our response.

We were understaffed, underfunded, underresourced, and overwhelmed. We wanted to do it all and do it well, and *no* was not in our vocabulary. I tried to push against unrealistic expectations when I thought it was called for, but my efforts rarely succeeded.

Every day we received messages from women who needed our help, from people who were likely struggling with mental health issues, and from men who hated us. The growing political divide in the United States was already visible in these messages as early as the mid-1990s. To keep from sinking into scorn and resignation, I tried to zero in on the hopes, fears, and impulses that all humans share.

What kept me there, even more than the mission, was the people. I worked with many, many amazing human beings who imparted to me several degrees worth of education about feminism, the intersecting issues of social justice, how government works, political strategy, coalition building, and how people tick.

We went out for lengthy happy hours full of griping, brainstorms, and laughter. Some of the funniest women I've ever met were (and still are) NOW women. Anyone who thinks feminists are dour and rigid has never hung out with us late at night at the hotel bar at a NOW conference. I'm not here to spill the tea, but as with many other workplaces, lots of drinking and hooking up took place. We worked extremely hard, and I know *I* felt entitled to play hard.

As you might guess, this led to some not so fine moments on my part. Experiencing a hangover-induced panic attack at the products booth at my first out-of-town conference is one that comes to mind. Wandering around outside a Las Vegas hotel late at night in a drunken haze and then stumbling into the hotel room where my roommate was trying to sleep is another.

Despite unpleasant memories like these, I am immensely proud of the work I did at NOW. It was there that I started truly believing in myself. I brought this new confidence in my skills and instincts to subsequent jobs.

When I left NOW, I promised myself that my days of mixing work relationships with excessive drinking were over, and I kept that promise. I also pledged that I would establish my own boundaries between work and life. My hunger for validation had driven me to overextend myself to the point that I resented both my employer and myself, and it needed to end.

My next job was a complete 180—an office where we had a huge marketing department and big budgets (at least in my mind). We worked with an advertising agency that hired models and actors to appear in our ad campaigns and shot TV commercials on soundstages and at beautiful rented homes (my mom even played an extra in one ad). And I was in shock that I no longer had to share a hotel room with someone when I traveled. What extravagance!

I did occasionally show up at the office dragging from a night of heavy drinking at home. Thankfully, while I was at that job, I finally gave alcohol the boot.

Alcohol had been eroding much of the self-confidence I was building up through my job performance. I couldn't perceive it then; now, I can see clearly how drinking consistently undermined the emotional development I was working so hard to achieve both inside and outside the office.

Once alcohol was removed from the equation, my personal growth began to accelerate, and my attitude toward my career took on unexpected dimensions.

After ditching my corporate marketing career in 2018, I took a part-time sales position at a fitness studio so that I could take my mom to dialysis and numerous other doctors' appointments. Working at a local business and performing outreach in the community offered me a new frame of reference. The studio held frequent member appreciation parties with adult refreshments, and I discovered the welcome relief of knowing I wouldn't be getting drunk and embarrassing myself around my boss, my coworkers, and our members. Those days were over.

Sobriety

"I'm thinking of starting a book club where we all sit around and drink wine and make excuses for why we didn't read the book. Who's in?!"

I posted this on my neighborhood Facebook page less than six months before I quit drinking. I went into sobriety convinced I was doing the right thing, and yet clearly my feelings about alcohol were complicated.

Those first couple of sober months were enlightening. I wasn't a heavy enough drinker to experience physical withdrawal symptoms or powerful cravings. The biggest issue was that abruptly an activity that had been a big part of my life was gone. I felt restless, irritated, and slightly adrift.

I read recovery-oriented books, blogs, and social media accounts in the daytime and listened to podcasts and guided meditations in bed at night. As soon as Aaron turned out the light and rolled over, I would pop in my earbuds and pull up the *HOME Podcast*. Eventually I would doze off, awaking with a jolt when the closing music started playing. Wide awake once again, I would attempt to find the spot in the show where

I had fallen asleep and resume play. I did this multiple times a night, the hosts' voices burning into my brain.

Some of the actions and events that I previously paired with drinking had to be put on hold, such as sitting by the firepit in the backyard that first summer (heck, it sorta sucked the next summer, too). Other activities—dining out, cooking, watching TV—required that I grit my teeth and slog through them without a glass or several of Pinot Grigio.

I rejected the lure of moderation. I did not want to be back in that space of constant negotiation with myself and my drinking, always disappointed in the end.

After those first couple of months, I started to adjust to the new routine. Which brings us to the next issue I had to tackle: fear of missing out.

My husband and my friends continue to drink. Amazingly, your peeps don't quit just because *you* did. Drinking is like an intense hobby, a seductive lifestyle that many people have no desire to abandon. I found myself touring breweries, wineries, and distilleries, watching others do tastings; going tubing down a river while everyone else drank beers; and turning down an offer to try a sip from a friend's fancy wine at a nice restaurant.

In none of these situations was I tempted to give in and imbibe in order to be part of the gang. But I did (and still do) feel separate when the people I love grow more and more loaded. At some point, inebriated people start to get a faraway look in their eyes. They are no longer fully with you—they have traveled to Drunkland, a realm inaccessible to sober folks. It can be lonely when you are the only person loitering on the outskirts of Drunkland.

(Quick aside: Perhaps this experience is payback for all those times my friends had to babysit me when I was a wasted mess.)

During lengthy drinking sessions, plastered people often experience energy bursts that allow them to stay up late and continue consuming. I remember well that ability to rally once another bottle of wine was opened. Sober me now likes to get to bed at a reasonable time. As I leave the gang to their revelry and turn in for the night, I am jealous.

Around the two-year mark of my sobriety, I was part of a group sitting at a bar eating dinner. Robin, who was quite buzzed, turned to me and said, "You know, just because you aren't drinking doesn't mean you can't have fun."

With some distance, it sounds like something *I* might have said back when I was drinking—a remark intended, I suppose, to get the sober person to lighten up.

At the time, though, I absorbed it as an insult. I considered several feisty comebacks, then settled for replying, as calmly as possible, "You're right."

I couldn't help wonder: Was I no longer fun? What the hell *is* fun, anyway—and who decides?

I've had plenty of fun without the supplement of alcoholic beverages. In fact, I respectfully propose that drunk people aren't as much fun as they think they are. Or, I think what's going on is that drunk fun and sober fun are two distinct kinds of fun that don't always mix.

Over the past five years I've been journaling and blogging about my transition from drinker to teetotaler. The subject fascinates me, and there's an elemental truth that I'm seeking.

Though I doubt I will ever ingest alcohol again, there's something I miss about drinking, even today. Alcohol was a pass into an exclusive club—a club literally *full* of people that nonetheless maintains a posh reputation. It was like the scene in the movie *Goodfellas* where they enter the restaurant through the kitchen. That's what drinking did for me—ushered me into a place, a state of mind, without having to wait in line. It allowed me to bypass my inhibitions. It was the "wind beneath my wings," until it became a hurricane.

But what if our inhibitions are there for a reason? What if we are meant to clamber up and over them using our raw faculties? Learning to move beyond my fears and hesitations without the leg up of alcohol is benefiting me in the long term. I'm building mental and emotional muscles that sat dormant for most of my adult life.

I'm convinced that there is nothing positive alcohol offered me that I can't conjure up myself. And that knowledge makes up for every moment of discomfort, FOMO, and party-pooper-itis.

Rediscovering Physical Activity

Around second or third grade some of the kids in my class came up with a weird schoolyard battle. At recess, a small group of us would line up at the monkey bars—the kind where there is a vertical ladder on each side, linked together at the top by a horizontal ladder of bars. If I recall correctly, this was a boy vs. girl thing. Only one boy competed in the game. He would climb up on one side, and a girl would climb up on the other side. Simultaneously, the two competitors would hang from the top on their respective sides and then move toward each other until they met in the middle, dangling from their arms and facing each other.

Both kids would then lift up their legs, each trying to be the first one to wrap their thighs around the other kid's waist and pull them down from the bars. It was all over in seconds, and then the next round began with the same boy and a new girl. I was one of the few girls who could typically beat that boy. Maybe because I was quick and limber. And being short actually gave me an advantage.

All I know is that school soon found a way to drain any youthful pleasure from physical activity. PE class became torture by focusing primarily on team sports. From that point forward, the kids in our class organically sorted into three general categories: the strongest and fastest kids who would go on to be football, basketball, and baseball stars throughout our school years; the perfectly adequate majority of the class; and the handful of us who were small, weak, or uncoordinated (or some combination thereof).

Unsurprisingly, when we picked teams in PE class, I was always one of the last kids picked. When a team captain would realize that their last pick was down to either me or some other poor sap, I could see them roll their eyes in disgust. Why did the coaches do this to us kids? Why not pick teams at random?

I could not hit a ball with a bat—that swish that happens when the bat misses the ball by a mile was an all too common sound of failure to me. I could not throw far or kick straight or run fast. We were playing kickball in sixth or seventh grade, and on my first up, I kicked the ball as hard as I could. It went right to the pitcher. I tried running to first base, and as I did, the pitcher ran alongside me holding the ball, waiting until I was inches away from the base to tag me.

Everything about physical education seemed designed to make sure I knew that I was pathetic. At this time, I was taking dance and gymnastics classes, so I knew my body was capable of grace and coordination. Once a year, we would do a short segment on gymnastics in PE, and I would get to show off my flexibility and balance. Sadly, those qualities didn't mean much in my school, as we didn't have a gymnastics team.

I spent many a class opting out of playing softball or flag football or basketball, slowly walking around the field or court with one or two other kids. Not all the coaches would let you do this, but some of them apparently understood how frustrating and humiliating it was for us weaklings. I still don't get why PE didn't involve more skill development, if the goal was for kids to learn how to move their bodies and find joy in physical activity. (Please tell me this has improved since I was a kid!)

In about eighth grade, we all had to do the Presidential Physical Fitness challenge, and one of the tasks was seeing how long you could hang from a bar in pull-up position. And what do you know, I was one of the better girls! For a few glorious minutes I was so proud. The fact that something so small has stuck with me all these years says a lot about the grim nature of PE class.

I did, as you know, go on to become a cheerleader in high school. We did not have a particularly athletic squad, so my modest gymnastics skills deteriorated.

Once I graduated high school, any lingering interest I had in fitness and sports immediately vanished. The girl who had loved climbing trees and hanging upside down on the jungle gym was gone. I blame it on PE class, drinking, and self-preservation. Who wants to remind themselves that they're physically inept? Maybe if earlier in my adulthood I had discovered yoga or something that suited my abilities, I would have taken to it. Instead, I discovered going out, drinking, and hooking up—and I was pretty good at those.

In my mid-twenties I went with a small group of coworkers on a white-water rafting getaway in upstate New York. The adventurous soul inside me had looked forward to it for weeks. On the car ride there, one of the guys on the trip implied that he didn't think I was going to be much help. Grrrr.

When we got there, we learned that the water level was really low because it was late in the season and there hadn't been much rain in weeks. Because of the low water, our raft kept getting stuck on the rocks, and one or two of us had to jump out each time and move us off the rocks. Partly to prove something to that guy, and also to prove something to myself, I jumped out of the raft more than anyone else and pushed harder than I could have imagined pushing. Every time I did this, I wanted to yell, *Did you see that, asshole? You're welcome!*

At the end of the trip, we all went to a bar where the

customers and the people who ran the rafting place all hung out and drank. I had never been so physically exhausted in my life; my arms and legs were like trembling leaves. That guy, whose name I have long since forgotten, came over and told me how impressed he was with my contribution in the river. I was smugly satisfied. Even better, I was thrilled to discover that I still loved pushing my body to its limits and testing my ability to overcome my fears.

In sobriety, this is something I have gravitated toward. Since quitting drinking, I have discovered that I love Pilates, aerial yoga, zip-lining, and Thai bodywork (on the receiving side). As an added benefit, exercise often takes me out into nature. I have been hiking amidst the trees and kayaking and paddleboarding on the water, and the positive effects have been immense. Being in the natural world helps me unplug, destress, and recharge.

The zip-lining I've done has been part of "treetop" obstacle courses. This involves navigating across unsteady bridges from one tree to another, with me shaking and grabbing on for dear life the entire time.

During my first zip-line adventure, I encountered the Tarzan swing, where you have to basically hurtle yourself through the air like a pendulum toward a big vertical cargo net. You are attached to a cable above your head, so you can't fall to the ground; nevertheless, it demands a sense of abandon. The people who had gone before me cheered me on and counted me down, and then I jumped. Right after I leapt, a friend who was on the ground snapped a picture of me using her zoom lens, and the look on my face is one of pure terror. But it might be the most fun thing I've ever done.

I'm so glad that later in my life I've made it a priority to try new things and to get back in touch with my athletic side.

When you're drinking on a routine basis, it takes up a lot of time and headspace. Your brain on alcohol can be a very static or regressive place to be. Like playing the same song over and over, the same stories get told again and again. The same grievances and insecurities are revisited.

Being in your body gets you out of your mind. The women at the Pilates studio I worked at several years ago often talked about how Pilates class was better than therapy—when they were on the equipment (called a reformer) and following the instructor, everything else would fall away. They could forget about work and other responsibilities for fifty minutes and just move.

One of my jobs at the studio was to convince new women to purchase monthly memberships. I felt such a kinship with the women who walked in that door. Many of them were middle-aged and had not thought much about exercise in forever. I bet *they* used to play and run and jump when they were kids, and then the appeal of movement drained out of them as it did with me.

Some of these women fell in love with Pilates instantly. I was touched whenever I saw a woman take to it—to start enjoying moving and challenging her body.

It was not unusual for someone who had never done Pilates to schedule an introductory class and then get cold feet. I'll never forget one woman who called to cancel because she got nervous. I encouraged her to stop in at the studio on her way home from work to observe an ordinary class, so she did. One of our members sat down with her on the bench up front as they watched the final ten minutes of a class. The member told this woman that *she* had been scared her first time, too— that she had been worried she would embarrass herself in front of the other women. We both assured this woman that all that fear would disappear as soon as she started gliding and stretching on the reformer.

The woman never came back to our studio. I reached out to

her several times after that, and I let her know that the member she had met that evening was offering to take the intro class with her. Even that wasn't enough to break through the wall this woman had put up between herself and physical activity.

One of the other passions I discovered after quitting drinking was aerial yoga, which involves hanging from a long, U-shaped piece of material (a "silk") suspended from the ceiling. It looks intimidating but is quite fun and safe. Whenever a new person in our class tried hanging upside down for the first time, I was secretly excited. I would watch as the instructor talked the newbie through it and stood by their side to spot them. Once this person got up the nerve and successfully flipped their feet up into the air and their head down toward the ground, I got a tingle all over and wanted to clap with glee for them. I was so proud of this stranger for trying something that they never would have thought their body could do.

Experiences like these, where we challenge ourselves physically and witness our own progress, build confidence. An old story I used to tell myself was that indoor cycling (a.k.a. spin class) was not for me. Guess what? In the course of finishing *My Unfurling* I found a studio that teaches a cycle class that I love, and I rewrote that outdated story.

I hate that so many of us miss out on this joy (yes, I said it, joy!) for so long. Many of us learned as kids that fitness means athletic competition in sports where we always come up short. There is so much more to it than that.

I would not have discovered the powerful tonic of movement and nature had I not stepped away from the bottle, the television, and the other decades-long habits that I thought defined me.

Meet Jill and Nora

On Christmas Day a couple of years ago my husband and I planned to make a seafood lasagna recipe that we reserve for special occasions. That morning I realized we had mistakenly bought a container of creamy goat cheese instead of goat cheese *crumbles*, and I insisted that it makes a difference. So, after opening presents, we drove around looking for an open grocery store. We found one, and then on our way home, I decided we should stop at a gas station to buy whole milk for the sauce so we wouldn't have to use my mom's lactose-free 1 percent milk.

We needed to get cracking as soon as we returned because, according to the timeline I had mapped out the day before, the process would take a total of two hours and forty-five minutes from start to finish.

Aaron was defrosting the shrimp in the sink when he called to my attention that the shrimp were already peeled. This recipe instructs you to use the shrimp shells to make a stock that is then used in the creamy sauce.

Well, I lost my shit. Standing there at the sink, I groped at the shrimp to confirm that they were shell-less. "Goddammit!" I yelled. "We just went out to the store and now this! I didn't even want to make this, but because it's *Christmas* we're supposed to cook something fancy!"

If you're feeling kinda bad for my husband, no worries. I feel bad for him, too—running around with me on Christmas Day and then having me scream at him.

You know what? It wasn't me screaming. It was freakin' Jill.

In the book *Burnout: The Secret to Unlocking the Stress Cycle*, by sisters Emily Nagoski, PhD, and Amelia Nagoski, DMA, the authors talk about "the madwoman in the attic." They explain that she is the "uncomfortable, fragile part of ourselves" who grew inside of us to manage the gap between who we are and who our families, friends, and society expect us to be.

Burnout encourages the reader to develop a persona (that got my attention!) for their madwoman in order to "separate yourself from her."

After reading that, I immediately started thinking about the woman inside of me, and the name Jill presented itself. Once she had a name, everything flowed quickly. And then Jill split off into another personality, Nora. So, let's get to know Jill and Nora ...

Jill is my inner glossy woman. She is the version of me that wants to be on reality TV, though she would surely be mortified by how I look on camera. Jill doesn't like my weight, except when the scale dips to an unsustainable number. She's the part of me that almost had an eating disorder.

Jill knows the exact four photos from my life in which I look pretty *enough*. She wishes I were taller with longer legs, firmer breasts, and a smaller nose. She has begrudgingly accepted my curly hair, yet wishes I would spend more time making it look nice. Jill hates my lack of enthusiasm for grooming practices; she gets extremely excited when I put on makeup or shave my legs. She *hates* how my neck looks now that I'm getting older.

Jill thinks I'm a competent writer but not particularly brilliant or scholarly; she's envious of writers she finds poetic and profound. She is disappointed that I'm not more classy, cultivated, or fashionable. Basically, Jill thinks I'm basic.

Jill wants me to be more ambitious and energetic. She's concerned that I won't achieve enough in life to make myself safe from criticism. She is not attuned to the fact that she is my biggest source of criticism.

Nora, on the other hand, is convinced that I was born with bad luck and that it follows me everywhere. Nora is very bitter about this state of affairs.

Nora does not like the fact that we humans don't have complete control over our lives. She thinks that as soon as one small thing goes wrong, it's going to snowball into an avalanche of awfulness and possibly end in abandonment or death. She is very much like the Debbie Downer character from *Saturday Night Live*.

Nora is sure that on top of my bad luck, I tend to do and say the wrong things a lot. She frets on my behalf that I'm going to do something stupid, so she's always warning me to brace myself for bad reactions from people.

Nora worries that people, even my good friends, will come to the conclusion that I am not a warmhearted or authentic or good person. She is afraid that I am easy to overlook and easy to forget.

Nora is the part of me that wants to hide under the covers and sleep for long periods.

A couple of days after my Christmas meltdown—the meal turned out fine, by the way—I was in the kitchen by myself, and I spilled some water. As it dribbled from the countertop down the cabinet door, I sighed, muttering, "As always, I made a mess."

Having just read the madwoman chapter of *Burnout*, I quickly said, "That was Nora talking. I don't always make a mess."

From that point on, I started saying, "Oh, that's Jill," or "There goes Nora again," when I get angry about trivial things, start panicking, or beat myself up.

This story demonstrates that I have pretty awesome timing, actually. That chapter of *Burnout* came along right after my seafood lasagna tantrum, when I was ripe for the lesson of personifying my inner critic. And thus, Jill and Nora were named, and I took another step in my journey.

My Unfurling

I often refer to my journey as an unfurling. I am unfolding, opening up, exposing facets of myself that were in hiding. Each stage of the unfurling reveals that there is more waiting to find the light. Often, I don't know what is waiting until it comes into view.

As a physical late bloomer in adolescence and now an emotional late bloomer in middle age, I am drawn to the symbolism of flowers blossoming and leaves uncurling.

Have you ever seen a time-lapse video of a fern sprouting and maturing (or read a description of it)? It is a mesmerizing process. First, the shoot emerges out of the dirt as if from nowhere. The slender stalk thrusts up toward the sky, and its tightly curled head starts to unwind. The fern grows taller, and the stem sways as the intricate fronds unravel and expand, one row after another. The end result is unexpected and improbably beautiful.

Whenever I try to locate the start of my second bloom, I find that I can jump back earlier and earlier. Quitting drinking in 2017 at the age of fifty-one was a major step that boosted my progress. But it wasn't the initial step. The year before that, I started my blog, which gave me a reason to want to quit, so I would have more time and energy for writing.

What if we were to look back a little farther? In the summer of 2014, when I was in my late forties, I became curious about eating healthier, and I started reading books on the subject, such as Michael Pollan's *In Defense of Food*, and *It Starts With Food* by Melissa Hartwig (now Urban) and Dallas Hartwig. This led me to do my first Whole30—an experiment in which I did not consume grains, dairy, added sugar, alcohol, or other designated foods or beverages for a full month. Those thirty days that September made me feel like a different, healthier person and showed me what life might be like without drinking.

Two years earlier, in August 2012, my husband Aaron and I bought and moved into a house on a lake. We almost didn't do it. We were terrified that we couldn't afford the mortgage payments and that we wouldn't be able to sell our townhouse. We took the plunge anyway, and it paid off in unexpected ways.

Living so close to nature made me calmer in general. It also made me want to be more active. Additionally, the move meant we were no longer crammed into a tiny townhouse with my mom, thus lowering my anxiety. And the greater distance from work contributed to my decision to leave my nonprofit job, which had been encroaching on my personal time and generating too much stress.

What about 2009, another landmark year? That fall, at the age of forty-four, I had a bad drinking experience that served as a wake-up call. On this occasion, I was out drinking with work friends on a Friday night, as we had done many times before. Something was shifting in my body—perhaps my metabolism or my hormones were changing. Whatever it was, I could no longer predict how quickly I would get drunk. I had had only a couple of beers that night and little or no food. I could feel myself drifting away as I lifted the third beer to my lips. The next thing I knew, I was on the train on my way home, almost at my stop. To this day, I don't know if someone escorted me to the metro station or if I walked there by myself and got on the train in a complete blackout.

I used to park my car at the train station and drive the last fifteen minutes from there to my house. I remember dumping the contents of my purse on the ground, but I could not find my car keys (thank goodness), so I had to hop in a cab. This was before Uber and before most taxis took debit or credit cards. So, late night trips like this often included the cab driver taking drunken me to an ATM to get cash.

At home, I pounded on the door; it was late, and my husband didn't answer. I walked around to the back of the house. Our kitchen deck was one story off the ground and had no steps, so I climbed up a tall ladder that was in our backyard and flung myself over the railing onto the deck. Once there, I tried throwing my purse and then my backpack up toward our bedroom window to wake Aaron up. My lumpy bags didn't hit the window with enough force, so I had to resort to throwing pieces of charcoal from our grill up at the window until I finally roused my husband.

Aaron came down to open the sliding glass door for me. I'll never forget the look of frustration and irritation on his face. My stepson was staying with us that night, and fortunately he did not wake up.

The next morning, I snuck out early to clean up the lumps of charcoal scattered all over the deck. I then had to call one of my friends from work—it was Saturday, and she was having a get-together with many of the same people from the night before. I made up an excuse, saying that I had forgotten Aaron and I had plans with my stepson. I could not face those people again. I was utterly ashamed. Having taken a guess that this friend was the one who had confiscated my keys, I thanked her and told her I would get them on Monday. Good guess.

I wasn't sure if our neighbors had heard me banging on the

front door, so when I ran into one of them the next day, I apologized in advance in case I had wakened them. I told them I had left my keys on my desk at work. Turns out the neighbors hadn't heard me, so there was no need for my fib.

After this event, I set some firm parameters for getting together with friends when I was solely responsible for getting my ass home. This time, I stuck to them. I even started going weeks at a time without getting drunk. The amount I was drinking crept back up when we bought the new house, but I think that tweak was the original inkling that an alcohol-free life might be in my future.

Earlier that same year, Aaron and I both quit smoking. The health risks were obvious, and we knew it was time. I was forty-three years old, and I had been smoking for twenty-eight years. Given my fear of dying from some horrific disease, it's incredible I smoked for that long. Over the prior year or two I had gradually cut down until I was barely smoking a pack a week, at which point my gynecologist asked, "Why don't you just quit?" So, my husband and I both quit in July 2009 and never looked back.

I could also point to when I started therapy for the second time, right before I met Aaron in January 2002, when I was thirty-six.

Or maybe summoning the courage to begin seeing my first therapist was the moment I first recognized that I had stopped flourishing. I don't remember that therapist's name; I looked through my files and couldn't find anything to confirm when I saw her. It was probably around 1997–98, when I was married to my first husband, Greg. She was a warm and fuzzy presence compared to my later, more exacting therapist. I was in my early thirties, and she was what I needed and was capable of handling at that point in my life. Our sessions ended because she moved away. When I shared this sad news with my friend Kelly, she told me she didn't think this therapist was doing me any good anyway! Brrrr.

I maintain that talking to that first therapist pulled ever so gently at the tangle of coping tools and distractions that were restraining me. You gotta start somewhere and somehow, right?

So, if you buy into this logic, then you'll agree that my second bloom began when I was about thirty-two. Meaning it took me another *two decades* to quit drinking after my emotional growth restarted! Do I wish I had quit sooner? You betcha. That's part of why I'm writing this book—in the hope that I will inspire someone to propel their own unfolding a little earlier than I did. And to let others know that this work can be done even if you feel that you've waited for way too long.

The biggest lesson I've learned is that you have to do something. And then another thing, and then another thing. Your milestones can be years apart, as evidenced by my timeline (1997, 2002, 2009, 2012, 2014, 2017)—as long as you're moving forward, no matter how slowly. There can be setbacks, as there was with my reinvigorated drinking in 2012. But I continued to be curious about my thoughts and my emotions and how they impacted my behaviors.

To step into a journey like this, you have to be ready to start looking at yourself. You can begin just beneath the surface, so long as you commit to delving deeper and deeper over time. You must be willing to experiment with changing your life. Sometimes it works best to start with a behavioral change, which can spark a subsequent emotional change. And sometimes you start with an adjustment to your mindset, and then the habit change follows. It is a beautiful cycle if you nudge it along, and when you look back, it all makes fantastic, perfect sense. Just like that fern.

Persona: The Crusader

As I grew up, I discovered another persona that appealed to me—the crusader. My religious family set the foundation for my attraction to being a do-gooder, and I took it in a different direction.

Around the age of ten, I shared with a neighbor that I wanted to be an ecologist when I grew up (this was the mid-1970s, and caring about the environment was gaining prominence). Our neighbor told me jobs like that weren't for girls and that I should think about being a nurse or a teacher. I was struck by the nonsensical limitations placed on women; I remember marching home to report to my grandmother how offended I was!

A couple of years later, my family was eating dinner and watching the nightly news when a segment aired about singer Anita Bryant, who was becoming known for her outspoken anti–gay rights activism. I innocently asked my family why Bryant had a problem with gay people. I don't recall their exact response; I do remember them being dismayed that I would even ask such a thing. I got the message that in our household we supported Bryant and that I shouldn't question her actions.

I'm not going to lie: Although helping people was part of the allure, what I really craved was an identity big and loud enough to shout over my insecurity. And being an advocate is just the kind of noble calling that marks one as a special, admirable person.

This desire to be a savior was intertwined with a longing to be seen as a martyr. For as long as I can recall, I have wanted people to feel sorry for me, to acknowledge my suffering, to apologize to me.

When I was a kid, one of my favorite games to play by myself was to imagine that I was sick in a hospital bed, and friends and family were coming to visit me. Or, I would flop myself onto the living room couch and pretend to be passed out. I would lie there as lifeless as possible, waiting for someone to come in and try to revive me. I usually lost patience before this happened. And no one ever responded with great concern, like I wanted them to.

As much as I felt sorry for myself, I was drawn to others who were also in pain. I was and still am fascinated with how we humans physically manifest our emotional suffering.

I loved reading books such as *The Best Little Girl in the World*, about a teen with anorexia (this was first drawing attention when I was a young teen), and *I'm Dancing as Fast as I Can* (which I borrowed from my mom), about a woman suffering from anxiety attacks and Valium withdrawal. Several years before I took my first sip of alcohol, and despite having zero drinkers in my family, I ordered a free booklet about alcoholism and intently read the quiz that would reveal if you were an alcoholic.

Sitting on a shelf in my bookcase is a collection of books about girls struggling with eating disorders, mental illness, drug addiction, abusive parents, and so on. Most of my early fiction writing is centered on emotional instability. Through my stories, I wanted to show readers that they were not alone. I also tried to comfort myself by creating characters in worse situations than my own. The novel I started for my senior year project in college, *The Way It's Supposed to Be*, was about an unhappy girl who goes in search of the mother who abandoned her.

My interest in politics began to bloom in 1980, when a classmate and I became obsessed with John Anderson, the independent candidate for US president that year. As I got older, I gravitated toward helping advance women's rights.

While living in New York, my friend Natalie and I started volunteering for NARAL Pro-Choice America. The 1992 presidential election was coming up, and we were handing out informational flyers outside subway stations. Over the next couple of years, we traveled to Washington, DC, to take part in reproductive rights and LGBTQ marches. The feeling of being part of something bigger than myself while being surrounded by like-minded people was intoxicating.

After moving to the suburbs of DC in 1995, I volunteered for an anti-violence rally and then went on to work for NOW, where I stayed until 2013. Through that job I met true heroes— inspiring leaders who were dedicated to women's equality and social justice.

Working at NOW was like being immersed in history as it unfolded. When relevant Supreme Court decisions came down, I was privileged to write the first drafts of NOW's press releases. At massive marches, I would walk backward with my camera in front of the front line to get photos of leaders and celebrities holding the long banner. I was there taking photos the day *Bush v. Gore* was argued before the Supreme Court in 2000.

I regularly worked outside normal office hours. I vividly recall taking the metro into the city on a Sunday evening after a major snowstorm for a scheduled *Roe v. Wade* candlelight vigil, then standing out in the cold for hours. I could have made more money and been less stressed working at a more ordinary job, but I didn't want to be ordinary.

In the end, I wasn't a crusader at heart. At least not the kind I envisioned when I heard the word—not like Susan B. Anthony, Harriet Tubman, or Rosa Parks. I did see people like this in action—the elected officers of NOW, leaders of other organizations, members of Congress—and they were mighty impressive. It was an honor to work for and alongside them for as long as I did.

After I left the nonprofit sector and stopped drinking, I was still drawn to the role of the reformer. When I discovered that a vibrant sobriety community was surfacing, my first instinct was to jump in with both feet and find a way to enlist the feminist movement in tackling recovery issues. My brain shouted: *This could be the next great social justice movement—and you could play a pivotal part in making it happen!*

I had to remind myself that I had tried on this persona and found it wasn't for me. My writing needed to be my focus. So, here I am, telling my story as my contribution to the world. And it feels right.

Six

TENDING MY GARDEN

Attitude Adjustment

As my habit of criticizing myself wanes, I'm keeping an eye on my tendency to criticize others. This may be the final frontier in my emotional development—refusing to let my inner judge run wild.

Throughout *My Unfurling*, I've portrayed myself as the object of what I've come to think of as "casual bullying." What I haven't covered much is my own part in teasing and mocking others. Writing this book conjured up moments that begged me to take a second look at my complicity in the same behavior that I found painful when directed at me.

It's hard to draw the line, though. At what point does playfully busting someone's chops turn into something callous and unkind?

Years ago, my friends and I were watching a movie together, and a young woman on the screen was primping and posing in the mirror. Several of us cried out in unison, "Look, it's Shannon!" Even Shannon had to laugh. Harmless, right?

But what about this? While I was living in New York City, several of us created a fictional TV show about our lives called *twentysomething* (inspired by the show *thirtysomething*, which was a cultural phenomenon in the late 1980s). Our imaginary show had no script or actual video footage. It simply consisted of us periodically declaring: "In tonight's very special episode, the gang gets drunk again."

In our ongoing attempt to amuse ourselves, we had a running gag that *twentysomething*'s ratings were down and something dramatic needed to happen. A couple of us, including me, periodically threatened to kill off a friend (a woman who does not appear in this book). I guess I was relieved not to be the butt of the joke for a change, so I enthusiastically participated.

The bit went something like this:

"The network says you have to die in a fiery crash in the season finale."

"Wait, what?! That's not fair!"

"Sorry, you're the viewers' least favorite character. You've got to go. It's for the ratings."

"You guys suck!"

"It's just a joke, you know. The show's not real."

I don't think it matters that this friend could be difficult. If she was anything like me, her feelings were hurt when teasing crossed the line into taunting. Eventually much harsher words were exchanged, and she and I haven't spoken in more than fifteen years. Looking back, what once seemed funny now feels cruel.

These days, my animus has an all-too convenient target: social media. Facebook, Instagram, Twitter, TikTok, YouTube— they're full of people who put themselves on display every day. Who could blame me for snickering at the guy who posts nothing but out-of-focus photos, or the woman who is obviously using her boobs to attract followers? What about all those poor people with no rhythm who keep making dance videos?

I force myself to look away from Instagram's suggested posts and videos, otherwise I will spend entirely too much time tsk-tsking at celebrities and influencers who, in my opinion, wear too much makeup, follow every damn trend, and go overboard with filters and cosmetic surgery.

On Facebook, I had to stop following two women in particular because I was reading their bewildering posts in the same way that I used to read the *Family Circus* comic, with a smug sense of arrogance.

For me, getting off on the cluelessness or vanity of others is usually a sign that my own ego could use some boosting. The thing about looking down on others is that it doesn't build any kind of permanent confidence. You must continually practice the art of the sneer to secure the cheap payoff of fleeting superiority.

As I was writing this book, I started reviewing the social media accounts, websites, and newsletters of self-published authors. I was doing this for inspiration and ideas, but I could find my jealousy kicking in and curdling into judgment. These folks, no matter how much I might disagree with their tactics, had already published their own books—in some cases many books—and it made me feel insecure.

It's not like I post nasty comments on anyone's feeds. All of this scorn takes place inside the privacy of my own head. And that is not a good thing. Plucking those thoughts from my brain requires watchfulness and effort. Fortunately, this attitude adjustment clears space for constructive thoughts about my own work, which in turn helps build the confidence I seek.

Sometimes I feel like a killjoy, like I'm going soft. But being hard and cynical isn't the answer. I'm proud that in writing *My Unfurling* I've looked at my own words and actions with an open mind and heart, attempted to learn something, and then committed to doing better.

Personal Values

Once I quit drinking, I started treating my life like an important assignment. One of my specialties in the workplace was managing long-term projects with lots of moving parts. Why not put that skill to work on the biggest project of all? (Me.)

In the branding work I've done for my employers, our "core values" existed not only to explain our identity to customers but also to help guide internal goal-setting and decision-making. So, a couple of years ago, I decided to develop my own personal values.

After compiling an extensive list of principles, characteristics, and behaviors that call to me, I grouped them into six overarching values: integrity, evolution, curiosity, balance, connection, and self-respect. These values now serve as a framework on which to hang my desires, my aspirations, and my progress toward positivity.

Here's a closer look at each one:

Integrity

I was raised to be honest and thoughtful and principled—traits I continue to hold dear. I was also raised to go to church, read the Bible, and follow a rigid set of rules that would get me into heaven.

Whereas most of the members of my family found a road map for integrity (they might call it morality) from within their strong belief in Christianity, I found it in my regard for other human beings and my desire to make a difference in the world. Through my work in political advocacy, I learned a great deal about fairness, opportunity, and justice.

In 2020, a former intern from my days at NOW posted on Facebook about the pandemic shutdowns. She revealed that she was having a tough time relating to "women who are insisting that the country reopen so that they can go to hair salons and get their hair dyed and styled."

She explained why she found this attitude difficult to sympathize with, and then she proceeded to demonstrate exactly how to empathize in spite of the difficulty. This woman asked herself a series of questions that allowed her to picture being in someone else's shoes. It was such a masterful example of how to open yourself up to another person's situation and background.

Challenging myself to follow this example is integrity. Seeing beyond my own narrow set of experiences is integrity. When I hear myself asking, "Why didn't she do it *this* way?" (meaning *my* way) or "Why did they do *that*?" (as in, something I would *never* do), integrity is what makes me stop and try to use my imagination to answer those questions for real. The answer might be something I can relate to after all.

Integrity is what encourages me to ditch jealousy and bitterness in favor of compassion and gratitude. It leads me away from selfishness and toward generosity. Integrity helps me put disappointment and resentment behind me and choose acceptance and grace.

Evolution

Over the past couple of years, the term *adulting* entered our cultural lexicon. Suddenly, loads of people were confessing, "I don't feel like adulting today."

Though it marks me as uncool (gasp!), I do not mind telling you that I am *down to adult.* Having been raised by a mom with a complicated relationship to adulting, I grew to appreciate responsibility, maturity, and seriousness. I see adulting not just as doing chores and other mundane tasks, but also as taking on the challenge of living one's life in an open-ended state of renewal.

About twenty years ago, I bought a pretty little book in a Pottery Barn or some such store. *The Art of Growing Up: Simple Ways to Be Yourself at Last,* by Véronique Vienne, is an easy, delightful read and contains a lot of wisdom. In the introduction, Vienne asks, "Could it be that each new stage and each new situation in life is an opportunity to shed youthful insecurities, reevaluate old habits, and get rid of obsolete constraints?"

She states, "The second part of your life is not a battleground. Growing up has a lot to do with making things easier on yourself. Like not dramatizing ... Apologizing rather than making excuses. And figuring out what you do best—and then doing it."

Not long before I hit my first year of sobriety, my husband and I went out to dinner. I asked the waiter what alcohol-free drink options they had and ended up ordering a strawberry lemonade.

"You know, I don't think you needed to quit drinking. I never thought you had a problem," Aaron said.

"Do you think I would have taken that writing class or started doing Pilates and yoga if I was still drinking?" I asked.

He sighed, "Probably not."

"Well, I think *that's* a problem—that I wasn't doing the things I wanted to do."

I think many of us are afraid that if we start changing our thoughts and actions it will be an indictment of who we are now and who we have been. Maybe that's why we get stuck: we become convinced we need to stay the same in order to validate who we are. But what if a big part of who we are is in hiding?

Personal evolution is a way of life—reflecting, welcoming the discomfort, and finding a way to move forward. *My Unfurling* is a testament to the value of evolution.

Curiosity

I've always been curious. Some might say nosy. But curiosity is about way more than wondering what other people are up to and questioning why they do the things they do.

Before I started drinking and trying to be hip, I was a dork. I liked school. I liked reading and learning and getting good grades. When I was a kid, the *Consumer Information Catalog* was a big thing. This free government-produced publication was like the internet of its time. Goofy TV commercials plugged the booklet, and I enthusiastically wrote to their address in Pueblo, Colorado. Once the catalog arrived, it was full of addresses and toll-free numbers that I could contact to request brochures on all kinds of subjects. I could not wait to check the mail each day to see if something new had arrived.

As I've embraced my curiosity again more recently, I've discovered that it extends to a sense of adventure that was waiting to be indulged all these years. Now I love trying new things to stimulate myself physically and mentally—like indoor rock climbing, tai chi, pole dancing, indoor skydiving, and online courses.

I also tap into my curiosity to explore human nature. I've spent a lot of time reading, contemplating, and writing about how humans are more alike than different, challenging myself to find what unites us.

I remind myself to make time and space for creativity, inquiry, and experimentation. If something is not working one way, why not try another way? And then another way! Keeping my mind active and probing makes me feel alive.

Balance

For eighteen years, I worked at a super demanding job. I took phone calls from the press late at night and on weekends, frequently dropping everything to hammer out a news release and arrange interviews for our president with media outlets. We were constantly cycling through staff on my team. Every time someone left for a new job, I had to take on the duties of the open position while identifying an impressive candidate willing to accept the modest salary we were offering.

I was working from home in the fall of 2012 when our press secretary called to inform me that she had accepted a job on Capitol Hill. The US presidential election was several months away, which meant I was going to be on press duty round the clock. I went to my bathroom, stepped into the shower, turned on the hot water, and cried and cried—big, gasping, heaving sobs. I was completely burnt out, and it was way past time for me to move on.

My shaky self-esteem and good-girl complex had long kept me in situations like this beyond what was emotionally and physically healthy. Throughout my adulthood, I paid a lot of lip service to the concept of balance. But I didn't actively foster it until years after I left the advocacy field, when I realized that I hadn't properly recovered from my burnout.

The recipe for balance varies from person to person. For me, I have to pay close attention to my body and my mind to uncover my needs, and then I have to act on those needs. I have to experiment with big actions, such as leaving a job, and smaller actions, such as giving up to-do lists. I have to spot my old patterns when they crop up and dispel their power.

I still say "Okay, fine" when I want to say "No." I am reluctant to delegate tasks to others because they might not execute them the same as I would. (Isn't it funny how someone with so much self-doubt is also quite certain that she performs an endless array of things in the most perfect way?)

I am learning to pace myself, to go way slower than I ever thought would be comfortable for me. I'm learning to recalibrate my goals to fit my fluctuating energy levels. Like my evolution, balancing is an ongoing process.

Connection

Connection is usually one of the last concepts that enters my mind when listing my values. I guess it feels almost too easy to include. My friends and family and significant others have always been central in my life. Connection is like breathing to me. What exactly would I gain from reminding myself that connection is a core value?

As with so many things worth understanding, it helps to go wide and deep—beyond my tight circle—to answer the question.

For the longest time, I thought I would be the same shy, timid girl for my whole life. While I was working part time at the Pilates studio, I discovered that actually I like talking to new people and getting to know them. My shyness was a coping mechanism that finally wore out its usefulness.

When my dear friend Shannon died, I exchanged messages with former classmates, some of whom I hadn't communicated with in years. I also started working with an online therapist to process my rage. Then I joined a grief group that met by Zoom. I vented and laughed and cried with these women. We sent each other emails with links to books, podcasts, and TED talks. We started scheduling separate one-on-one calls in addition to our group Zooms. One of the greatest things I learned from these women was how to listen and ask questions and how to be present for others. I'm not saying I got great at it—I still want to jump in with my own stories as soon as someone takes a breath. Even so, I'm making headway.

My progress would be nothing if I didn't induce myself to be more attentive and loving toward others. Identifying what we all have in common—our shared fears and hopes—is the key to finding genuine connection with all human beings.

Self-Respect

The act of unfurling is the great work of my life. Awakening to my own worth and what it means to honor that worth is a revelation.

I've put all kinds of poison into my body. Dragged myself to work hungover and then snuck in a nap under my cubicle desk. Screamed awful things at my closest friends. Begged people to love me or fool around with me. Cheated on partners and had sex with people who were married or in serious relationships. Gossiped, stole, lied, vandalized.

In the background, my mind was at war. My selfish side wanted all the things with no consequences. My puritanical side was terrified I was going to hell, if there was such a place.

As I matured, a third side emerged, a woman who understands what the girl went through. A woman who can be forgiving while still expecting better for herself. A woman who has her own back in every sense of the phrase. A woman who loves herself.

In her book *You Belong: A Call for Connection*, author and meditation teacher Sebene Selassie writes, "When we truly love ourselves, we don't need to be someone or something else. When we love ourselves, our sense of separation softens, the need to dominate dissolves. Comparison and competition clear away in the presence of self-love. Hierarchy and oppression crumble. We belong."

Sitting down at my computer, writing and editing this book —even when Jill and Nora were telling me that it probably wouldn't be published, that I'm just a self-indulgent, mediocre writer with nothing special to say—that's self-respect.

Holding my own hand, always, with pride and responsibility and conviction. That's self-respect.

Finding What Works

Using my values as fertile soil, I am always on the lookout for actions, attitudes, and approaches that work for the life I am cultivating. Tending to a fulfilling life is no small job, so I feel it is my duty to share the practices that have become essential to my "thrivival" (yeah, it's hokey, but so am I).

The items in my toolbox won't work for everyone. That said, perhaps some of them will spark ideas that you, dear reader, can make your own.

These tactics may morph as my journey progresses, but I think the essence of each one is both flexible and enduring. Let's do this!

Know Thyself

For me, sobriety was the linchpin in getting to know myself. For others, it may be something else. You know how in tales about haunted houses there's often a locked door with a missing key? Well, it took me decades to figure out that my missing key was quitting drinking. Once I got that door open, I found so much illumination waiting for me, as well as other doors to pry open. I had a whole separate wing of my psyche to explore! Getting to know myself provides much-needed context for my personal stories, a fresh outlook on my actions, and permission to disengage from behaviors that are black holes for my time and energy.

Looking within and rigorously (yet kindly) questioning yourself is a healthy priority. I'm not talking about letting your inner critic torment you. I'm suggesting that it's okay to contemplate whether your current behaviors are serving you well. We shouldn't get down on ourselves; neither should we shrink from examining our routines and our most durable attachments. We can love and accept ourselves *and* confront the thoughts and actions with which we've grown comfortable.

We all like to stay safe and not provoke ourselves—it's a feature of being human. When we get overly defensive, we may have exposed ground that's ripe for exploration. And if something in our lives can't handle a respectful interrogation, maybe it needs to go.

One of the ways we get to know ourselves is by trying out a variety of pursuits. Locating the door that is in the way and unlocking it is vital to self-discovery. I'm glad that I didn't wait for some rock bottom that may have never come. I recognized the potential contained within sobriety and followed it through the doorway.

Habit Shifting

All the other closed doors that materialized after I quit drinking represented a collection of bad habits and counter-productive behaviors that had become part of my operating system. Day after day we make small, barely conscious choices. Acknowledging them is critical. Throughout the day, I remind myself to stop and think before I act, to make mindful choices about how I spend my precious time. It is said that time is money, but I think it's even more serious than that. Your time is a resource that you can't get back.

About a year ago, I created a list with two columns. On the left were all the actions I was doing automatically with little urging, and on the right were the actions I struggled to do on a consistent basis, despite my desire to do them. In the left column, I looked for items I could scale back, delegate, or give up entirely so that I could open up time for some of the items on the right. I elected to stop watching cable news because it was stressing me out and commandeering brain space (another vital resource of ours). Given a choice between scrolling through social media or reading a book, I started choosing the book. When I have a few minutes to spare, I try to journal, do something crafty with my hands (which is not a strong aptitude of mine), or research self-publishing.

In general, I am making a deliberate effort to create more and consume less. Gradually, I have been venturing away from screens and other people's products and giving my mind space to produce its own creations. Yes, I still watch TV and check out social media, but they have moved farther down on my priorities list. I accepted that giving them up was the easiest way to get other stuff done.

Slowly, I am forming new habits and shifting the old ones from automatic to optional. The clue is to stop and think first before acting on instinct.

Jumping In

I know there are people who jump into doing risky and/or expensive things without much thought or planning. I am not one of them. For ages, I would say I wanted to do something new and exciting. Then I would find a million things to do first, or I would completely overthink my decision until I lost interest or the opportunity expired. It wasn't yet evident to me that I was, in fact, *choosing* not to leap. Because my powers of procrastination are so strong in this area, I have created an exception to my stop-and-think rule. Now, when an intriguing online class becomes available or I get a sudden hankering to try indoor skydiving, I give myself a hall pass to jump in with only minimal deliberation. If I don't hit fast-forward periodically, I won't get to live the life I want.

Meditation / Mindfulness

I confess that I'm not particularly good at meditating, nor do I practice as often as I'd like. Nonetheless, it has been hugely beneficial in multiple areas of my life. I'm convinced it has helped me calm down in general and live in the moment. In addition, some of the skills I've learned from meditation are helping me sleep better, which is absolutely crucial to feeling my best.

Not long ago, I rolled over to go to sleep and my body recognized this trigger and went into fear-of-death mode. (This continues to be a thing for me.) My heart turned into a boulder rolling at breakneck speed down a steep hill, and I could not catch it. Instead of letting the feeling of panic engulf me, I started my twenty-two-second breathing exercise: breathe in, feeling the air fill my belly, while counting from one to seven seconds; hold my breath from eight through ten; breathe out for the count of eleven to twenty; hold for twenty-one and twenty-two; then start all over again at one. Within several cycles of breath, the hill under the boulder levels out and I relax. Usually, I'm asleep within five minutes of initiating this exercise. If not, I move on to grounding—I focus on my body, how it feels in the places where it touches the bed, and how the covers and pillow feel against my skin. These techniques work at all times of the day to diminish anxiety or annoyance. And the more I do them, the better they work.

I think many people still see meditation as this hippie or New Agey thing that doesn't have anything to offer them. A couple of years ago, I took an online training in Unified Mindfulness, which helped me look at meditation as a skill. And it's not an exaggeration to say it changed my life.

By accepting that thoughts can come and go without my full endorsement, I have made huge strides in loosening my grasp on anger and self-pity. Times arise when all I want to do is roll around in my negative emotions. The good news is that the more I meditate, the easier it gets to resist such wallowing.

Movement and Nature

My habit shifting has included gravitating toward nature and moving my body. I see the two as linked because being outdoors makes me want to be in motion, to nurture my physical strength, agility, and flexibility.

The terms *working out* and *beach body* don't appeal to me, though I understand the importance of regular exercise. Finding a form of movement that works for you might take time and lots of trial and error. Pilates, yoga, and cycling make me happy, but I still have to push myself to do them.

I miss the dancing I did as a girl, so I've been looking for a dance class that will fulfill this longing. I also have my eye on a course that promises to connect my writing with my body and nervous system. I'm telling you, there is an endless world of options for movement on the internet—especially now that so many classes have online offerings.

The beauty of movement, nature, and being in touch with my senses has become an important tool for getting out of my chaotic head. Speaking of chaos …

OCD Tencencies Management

This section might be the most specific to my personal brain chemistry. Still, I am confident that there are others out there like me with a busy airport for a brain who will appreciate these tips. By the way, this part could probably be a book of its own, so I'll try to be brief.

My to-do lists are no longer obsessively long and detailed —the only items that go on them are doctors' appointments and other activities that involve a scheduled commitment. Initially, I took a break from making *any* to-do lists, and it offered a peek into what I really wanted to do with my time. I had to get comfortable with forgetting some things, which meant learning to put them in perspective. It turns out that not everything is a big deal.

Numbers are my kryptonite. Every day, I face the urge to count, track, measure, or time things that do not need to be counted, tracked, measured, or timed. Standing up to this urge clears my head and relieves unnecessary pressure. While there are a few areas where this can't be avoided, there are many, many cases where I was counting because it had become deeply ingrained.

For a long time, I had this vision that it was possible to complete a bunch of minor tasks and then relax with the knowledge that nothing was hanging over my head. I now know that this vision is an utter fantasy, so I've stopped tackling all the tedious stuff in advance to get it "out of the way." It's a hard impulse to break, so I have to check in with myself and do the things I want or need to do first. It is up to me to make time to chill, or have fun, or just go to the bathroom already, dammit!

Lowering your standards can be amazingly liberating. (Say what?!) At first it felt very wrong, so I had to coach myself through the process. I admitted that I was turning trivial chores into complicated, time-consuming projects. I had to start asking myself questions, such as:

- What would happen if I saved the laundry for later?
- Must I track our finances manually when there are like a gazillion tools for this very purpose?

- Can someone else help with the yard work or take it over altogether?
- Am I being paid to clean toilets at a master level?
- Can I scratch my itch for order in a more creative way than reorganizing the dishwasher?

Talking to yourself can be a good thing, but I have a penchant for retelling myself the same stories. I relive bad experiences, revisit old grievances, catastrophize, and imagine arguments. Even reciting positive stories, such as the steps that led me to quit drinking, can eat up time better spent generating new thoughts. If I don't interrupt and replace these internal scripts, they will keep running on autopilot.

As time goes on, and with concerted effort on my part, my obsessive-compulsive tendencies have become less prominent. I am amazed at how much calmer, more spacious, and more creative my mind feels.

Accepting My Pace

When I left my most recent full-time job at the age of fifty-two, I did so with the knowledge that I no longer wanted to play office politics or climb the corporate ladder. I had ascended as high as I wished, and I was surprisingly okay with the fact that I would never be a VP, let alone an executive director or CEO.

For so long, I thought I needed to be more driven. What I actually needed to do was accept that I *wasn't* super ambitious —that some of the fuel I had been operating on at work was made up of insecurity and a need for affirmation.

Our culture values initiative, diligence, and productivity. We often look down on those we think aren't living up to their potential or to society's expectations. I've been guilty of this myself—thinking that people are being lazy and taking advantage of others.

Now I'm looking at this from a new standpoint. We already

know that people are different in all kinds of ways. Maybe we are also different in our ability to grind.

Maybe some of us were meant for a slower life. Maybe some of us get stressed out more easily than others. Maybe it's okay if we don't all work at the same speed and intensity. Maybe some of us need longer sabbaticals in between periods of steady employment.

Accepting one's own pace can be tricky. We have to function in a society that rewards energy and enterprise. And we all need money to survive. At the same time, there are lots of little moments in our lives when we can pause and let ourselves off the hook.

For example, seeing people post multiple times a day on social media was making me feel like a loser. Instead of posting more, though, I started scrolling less, and I found that my fear of being irrelevant faded away.

To all those people with energy to burn, I salute you! But to those of us who have been faking it until we make it (a phrase I've never liked): It's okay to slow down.

Giving Up on Winning

News flash: You don't have to win every argument. You don't even have to try. You can let disagreements be disagreements, nothing more. I have dodged this lesson for ages.

Social media put my propensity for bickering on full display. Arguing over politics in the comments was a compulsion of mine. I would debate with anyone in an attempt to win the argument and prove to myself that I was the bestest debater there ever was. I would read what I thought was a stupid opinion, and even before I typed the first word of my reply, I could feel the blood rush to my temples as I formulated my case. I could spend a full day going back and forth with the same person—sometimes it was someone I didn't even know. And I took these fights seriously—I could feel my heart racing each time my opponent refused to concede.

I worked on restraint through sheer willpower, which got me about 50 percent of the way there. Then, a couple of years ago I turned off all social media notifications on my phone. Next, I removed nearly every social media app from my phone (especially you, Facebook). I still have to mentally drag myself away from a quarrel now and then, but the difference in my anxiety level is astounding. Not to mention the time I have reclaimed.

Of course, I've been known to get into a row with a friend over text, too. The brilliant thing is that later I can scroll back through a text fight and see the exact point at which I should have stepped off but didn't. Reviewing these squabbles on-screen has been helpful for identifying my triggers and making plans for how to exit early and more gracefully next time. I still often go one or two remarks farther than I'd prefer, but I'm making progress.

The "Why" Exercise

When something gets under my skin, I've started asking myself why it bothers me so much. My first answer is just a shallow starting point. I keep asking a series of *"But why"* questions (like a little kid would) until I reach something that feels uncomfortably true. Here's an example:

Why did you get upset when Robin didn't reply to your text today?

I guess I expect close friends to respond to my direct messages.

You know that even close friends don't reply to every text. Why did this time bother you?

I thought she would find it funny, and I was looking forward to her reaction.

Why was her reaction so important?

It's nice to know you can make your friends laugh.

Maybe she didn't find it as funny as you did. Why is that difficult to accept?

Even if it didn't make her laugh, she could have at least responded.

Why did her response matter?

I realize people have stuff going on in their lives, and they don't have time to respond to every silly message. But I take things like that personally. I saw this quote recently: "No response is a response." That really struck a chord.

Why did it strike a chord?

My brain often makes the jump from a single comment being unworthy of a response to *me* being unworthy of a response. So, I start to worry that my friend doesn't like me anymore.

After all the self-development work you've done, why is it still difficult to believe in yourself?

Because those old storylines of unworthiness are still imprinted in my head.

[Having reached this nugget, the last question switches to a more active approach.]

So, how are you going to flip the script?

By stopping these thoughts in their tracks, refusing to engage with them, and replacing them with more rational thoughts.

As you can see, this exercise often takes me back to one of my old insecurities. Exposing this chain to the past and then forming a plan for breaking the chain is crucial to my unfurling.

Boundaries

There's a reason I left boundaries for last, and it's the same reason it has become such a buzzword in our culture. Boundaries are freakin' hard. I think we all wrestle with them in at least one area of our lives.

During the years I worked at NOW, I supervised many people. One woman came to work on time and left on time and worked hard while she was there. She was nice, but she was not one for copious socializing. When she went home at the end of the day, she was off the clock. I don't recall her making a statement to this effect; we just knew it. I felt bad for those who followed her in that position because many of them worked late and from home when necessary. This was due, in part, to the world changing and technology making it easier to work from home at all hours. Still, this woman knew something about establishing boundaries. What the heck was her secret?

I don't have any magic tips for setting and maintaining boundaries. I grapple with them all the time. I do think recognizing their importance is half the battle.

One maneuver I've been putting to the test: When someone asks me to do something that I can't completely turn down, I negotiate for something in return or for an adjustment to the request that will better suit my capacity level. This simple act of calling for a compromise makes me feel more in control.

Release

In childhood, I learned how the fragility of one person's psyche could crowd out the needs of another. For most of my life, "mother first" was the unspoken custom. In middle age, I still struggle to refrain from always putting her needs (which, on occasion, feel more like tests than needs) before mine.

Not long after my mom moved in with me and my husband, about ten years ago, she went away for a week to visit a friend. While she was away, I was at work and found myself doubled over with sharp stomach pain. It was bad enough that my boss drove me from our offices in Washington, DC, to an urgent care facility near my home in the suburbs of Maryland.

The doctor confirmed it was not appendicitis but said it might be diverticulitis, which can range from minor to severe. The pain was starting to subside, so we decided to take a wait-and-see approach.

When I called my mother to check in that evening, I told her what had happened and said that I was feeling much better. Twenty minutes after we hung up, Mom called back in a frenzied state. She had talked to her friend's daughter, who is a nurse, and now she was freaking out that something serious might be wrong with me.

I ended up getting my mom calmed down, but now I was pissed. This is how it often goes with Mom. She worries about other people's issues in a manner that turns them into her own issues. With unconscious guile, she positions herself at the center of the situation so that *she* requires attention and soothing. In a more recent episode, my mother crossed a boundary with an acquaintance that verged on an invasion of privacy (for that reason I won't go any farther, but it was bad enough that we had to have a talk).

My late friend Shannon—the other woman who plays a central part in this book—could not have been more different from my mother. Whereas my mom's emotions and hungers are right there on the surface, Shannon's were buried far beneath. I wanted so bad for Shannon to acknowledge that she could use some help, that she was afraid, and that she had a deep well of unmet needs that deserved attention.

Shannon was not needy enough. My mom is *too* needy. Make up your mind, Lisa!

Maybe I should be happy that my mother is the way she is, as exhausting as it can be. Sure, she's an emotionally "high maintenance" person—something that's totally uncool in our society. But it's also possible to make oneself excessively *low* maintenance, which sounds like a lonely road to walk.

As much as I'd like to feel superior to my mother in this area, I'm familiar with the motivation behind such melodrama —the way concern for a friend or family member can escalate to a feeling of panic and desperation. The primitive part of my brain is worried about being abandoned, while my ego craves approval.

Recently I butted into someone's life, and in the course of telling them they needed to get support for addiction recovery, I started lecturing their significant other on getting vaccinated. My concern for this couple became more about getting them to follow my advice so I would be satisfied that I was right. After my last several texts went unanswered, I forced myself to stop. In retrospect, I'm pretty sure I crossed the threshold from caring to annoying.

This leads to my final conclusion: We can educate, bargain with, and implore other people to change, but we cannot *make* them change. Also, we can sift through our own past and analyze what was done to us, but we cannot alter those things.

I've been looking for the right word to describe what I must do with my relationship with my mom. Is it love—do I need to love her more? Is it forgiveness—do I need to find a way to truly forgive her? Is it acceptance—do I need to accept that she did the best she could with the skills and tools she had?

All of these are fine, but actually it's not a word directed at her. It's a word directed at me, the person whose thoughts and actions I can shape.

It's *release*. Release is not about letting go entirely. It is about loosening my grip so that I don't continually recycle my own anxiety, anger, and sadness. Release is a gift to myself, and by extension a gift to my mom and everyone else affected by my state of mind.

I don't know if this will work. All I can do is try and see what happens. For now, I will:

- Release disappointment.
- Release resentment.
- Release my craving for validation.
- Release the need for others to follow the script in my head.
- Release my longing for wholehearted apologies from those who have hurt me.
- Release the desire to bend others to my will.
- Release the notion of perfection.

Writing *My Unfurling* offered me the opportunity to cradle my delicate heart in my own hands, to begin healing the wounds that I've fussed over for so long. It presented me with the time and space to try on different points of view that brought context to my own behavior and that of others.

My perpetual unfurling is about so much more than staying sober and sampling a series of fun new activities (though both are excellent). It's about making deliberate decisions in my life, from small ones to big ones. It's about being kind to myself when it turns out that my decisions suck, or when I stumble or freeze up. It's about recognizing the abundance of options available in this world and experimenting mentally, emotionally, spiritually, and physically to see which ones work best for me.

Most of all, my unfurling is about finding the light so that I can bloom as many times as possible.

Persona: Me!

E very Tuesday I listen to Rachel Hart's *Take a Break from Drinking* podcast. Although I quit drinking nearly five years ago, this is the one sobriety podcast that remains in my weekly rotation. Hart's approach works for pretty much all aspects of life, and her show often nudges me back on track when I'm feeling down on myself.

In her two hundredth episode, entitled "Celebrating You 2.0," Hart talks about how "all of your thoughts are up for grabs"—especially those stories we tell ourselves about how inadequate we are.

Hart submits that "learning how to celebrate you is the key to habit change. It is not a nice add-on if you have some extra time. It's necessary. It's everything."

Standing in my kitchen, I heard those words at the right time. I was working on this book and worrying that it was mired in negativity. Hart's podcast convinced me that in writing this manuscript, I was starting a whole new relationship with myself.

The funny thing about exploring the personas I most admired for *My Unfurling* is that I finally began to see some of those coveted qualities in myself. I am a mix of the cool chick, the crusader, the creative genius, and the weirdo. Even tiny slices of the glossy woman and the sex enthusiast dwell inside me.

Some of my favorite traits in the cool chick persona are resourcefulness and self-sufficiency, which I am proud to claim for myself. Plus I am far more outspoken than I usually acknowledge. My shy girl days are definitely behind me. My self-confidence didn't burst forward like a birthright—I steadily and intently constructed my assurance and audacity. (Which is kinda awesome.)

I've had do-gooder leanings for as long as I can remember. While I don't fit the traditional mold of a crusader, I can't imagine committing myself to a career or a calling that doesn't involve helping people get closer to achieving their dreams.

The surface trappings of the creative genius eluded me, but through the process of writing this book I discovered that I still love stitching words together to communicate ideas. And I bring creativity to many of the things that I love to do, such as getting organized and building an intentional life.

I will always be a goofball. It doesn't matter that I didn't adopt any special kind of look or become immersed in a passion that might mark me as a true weirdo. If you get to know me, you will find that I'm a dork at heart. And I'm fully capable of acting downright silly without a drop of alcohol.

The glossy woman shows up from time to time when I get "all dolled up" (as one of our wacky friends in Manhattan used to say) to go out. And the sex enthusiast is in there cheering me on to not give up on getting genuinely comfortable with my sexuality.

There's a lot more to me than a handful of characteristics from some personas I've obsessed about over the years. It took me a long time to see the good in myself, to see that I didn't need to fit some specific role in order to be special. That I didn't need to be admired to be worthy. That I didn't need to be like a character from a book, a movie, or a TV show to be interesting. I just need to be me.

As I edited *My Unfurling* over and over, I picked up on how even the shy little girl, the insecure teenager, and the dormant adult kept doing things that scared them. In the introduction, I mentioned how frustrated I would get with myself whenever I let another gym membership lapse. What if I was focusing on the wrong side of that pattern? What if the real point was that I kept trying? The active, curious, adventurous part of me was in there striving to get my attention. She never gave up.

"Me" was hiding underneath a bunch of fears and coping devices and distractions. I had to be willing to sweep those aside to find her. And then I had to *be* her. I had to keep doing this over and over because interference and resistance runs deep in my veins. Being myself is a never-ending job, and it's the best shot I've got at true contentment.

About the Author

Lisa May Bennett is a repeat late bloomer who writes about personal growth and trying new things on her blog, *Bittersweet Nugget*. Lisa first decided she wanted to be a writer at eleven years old but struggled for years with self-doubt and anxiety. Now, she has published her first book at age fifty-six and hopes to serve as an example for others who wonder if it's too late to chase their dreams. (No, it's not.)

Lisa worked in the nonprofit sector for nearly two decades, serving as the communications director at the National Organization for Women for thirteen years. She also worked in TV ratings research in New York City and in marketing for an online education company. She is currently a caretaker, freelancer, and habit-development enthusiast.

She has lived up and down the East Coast of the United States and now resides on a lake in Maryland with her husband, her mom, two cats, and a dog. Lisa enjoys paddleboarding, yoga, and dancing in the kitchen. She plans to cross the country in an RV with her husband one day.

You can help other readers discover this book! Please rate and review *My Unfurling* on Amazon at mybook.to/myunfurling or by scanning this QR code. To grab your free *My Unfurling* bonus chapters and stay up-to-date on Lisa's projects, visit lisamaybennett.com and sign up for her newsletter.

Acknowledgments

I owe a huge debt of gratitude to my mom, my closest friends, and my husband—not just for allowing me to share personal recollections about them in these pages, but also for the decades of love and support they have given to me.

Educators are some of my earliest heroes. My interest in writing was nurtured by high school English teachers Diane Davis and Kathleen Long. College writing professor Andy Solomon recognized my promise, pushed me to elevate my craft, and became a dear friend.

A proposal for the original version of this book was conceived in a 2017 course led by author and publisher Anna B. David. Thanks to her, I started thinking of myself as a writer again. Anna and the course's book mentor, Kristen McGuiness, offered heaps of encouragement and input on that first concept, which eventually transformed into *My Unfurling*.

Once I started writing this version, Jessica Dixon served as my accountability partner, and her cheerleading kept me motivated and on track. Jessica was also one of more than fifteen test readers who provided invaluable feedback. I am eternally grateful to these folks for taking the time to read my book (or try to, in some cases) and to articulate what was and was not working.

Editor Christine Driver went above and beyond with her developmental critique, helping me address some of the structural issues raised by the test readers; and line editor/proofreader Sandy Brown performed an invaluable polish of the manuscript.

The members of the Maryland Writers Association, Self Pub Hub, and the Self-Publishing Support Group (on Facebook) were immensely helpful in the latter stages of editing and publication.

Authors Serena J. Bishop and Nonna Henry, who have self-published, provided great insight and information related to the process.

Indie author R.W. Harrison formatted the content of this book in addition to reviewing the manuscript and answering my endless stream of publishing and marketing questions.

Lastly, I wish to thank the family members of "Shannon" for understanding my desire to include the part of her story that intersected with my own. Shannon often spoke affectionately about her family, and I could not imagine publishing *My Unfurling* without honoring their loss. And thank you to Shannon for being a constant confidant and coconspirator for more than four decades.

Inspiration and Resources

Creativity and Journaling

Get Untamed: The Journal (How to Quit Pleasing and Start Living)—book by Glennon Doyle

Big Magic: Creative Living Beyond Fear—book by Elizabeth Gilbert

Magic Lessons (archives)—podcast hosted by Elizabeth Gilbert

Writing Down the Bones—book by Natalie Goldberg

On Writing: A Memoir of the Craft—book by Stephen King

What's Your Story: A Journal for Everyday Evolution—book by Rebecca Walker and Lily Diamond

Habits and Mindfulness

Atomic Habits: An Easy & Proven Way to Build Good Habits & Break Bad Ones—book by James Clear

Reset—online course and other offerings from Jocelyn K. Glei

Ten Percent Happier—app cofounded by Dan Harris

Ten Percent Happier, "How to Change Your Habits," episode #345, May 10, 2021, with Katy Milkman—podcast hosted by Dan Harris

The Creative Habit: Learn It and Use It for Life—book by Twyla Tharp and Mark Reiter

You Belong: A Call for Connection—book by Sebene Selassie

Don't Feed the Monkey Mind: How to Stop the Cycle of Anxiety, Fear, and Worry—book by Jennifer Shannon, Doug Shannon, and Michael A. Tompkins

Unified Mindfulness (free CORE training)—meditation program founded by Shinzen Young and Julianna Rae

Personal Development and Enlightenment

BetterHelp—e-counseling platform

Option B—online grief support

"The Power of Vulnerability" and "Listening to Shame"—TED talks by Brené Brown

Daring Greatly: How the Courage to Be Vulnerable Transforms the Way We Live, Love, Parent, and Lead—book by Brené Brown (really any of her books!)

Untamed—book by Glennon Doyle

Tell Me Something True—podcast hosted by Laura McKowen

Burnout: The Secret to Unlocking the Stress Cycle—book by Emily Nagoski and Amelia Nagoski

Inward and *Clarity & Connection*—books by Yung Pueblo

"The Communications Cure"—TED talk by Dr. Neha Sangwan

You Are a Badass: How to Stop Doubting Your Greatness and Start Living an Awesome Life—book by Jen Sincero

Wild: From Lost to Found on the Pacific Crest Trail—book by Cheryl Strayed

Tiny Beautiful Things: Advice on Love and Life from Dear Sugar—book by Cheryl Strayed

The Body Is Not an Apology: The Power of Radical Self-Love—book by Sonya Renee Taylor

Do the Thing, "Hypothangry," episode #40, August 18, 2020, with Dr. Vickie Bhatia—podcast hosted by Melissa Urban

The Art of Growing Up: Simple Ways to Be Yourself at Last—book by Véronique Vienne

The Nature Fix: Why Nature Makes Us Happier, Healthier, and More Creative—book by Florence Williams

Sobriety

Enjoli—essay by Kristi Coulter

Nothing Good Can Come from This—book by Kristi Coulter

This Naked Mind—book by Annie Grace

Take a Break from Drinking—podcast hosted by Rachel Hart

Drink: The Intimate Relationship Between Women and Alcohol—book by Ann Dowsett Johnston

Drinking: A Love Story—book by Caroline Knapp

"Am I an Alcoholic?"—essay by Laura McKowen (the piece that convinced me to quit)

We Are the Luckiest—book by Laura McKowen

HOME Podcast (archives)—podcast hosted by Laura McKowen and Holly Whitaker

"Gray Area Drinking" and NOURISH—TED talks by Jolene Park

Quit Like a Woman—book by Holly Whitaker

www.ingramcontent.com/pod-product-compliance
Lightning Source LLC
Chambersburg PA
CBHW030412130626
46549CB00004B/1737